# Fossil Fuels

## Energy and the Environment

ReferencePoint
Press™

San Diego, CA

# Select* books in the Compact Research series include:

## Current Issues

Abortion
Animal Experimentation
Biomedical Ethics
Cloning
Conflict in the Middle East
The Death Penalty
Energy Alternatives
Free Speech
Genetic Engineering
Global Warming and
    Climate Change
Gun Control
Illegal Immigration

Islam
Media Violence
National Security
Nuclear Weapons and
    Security
Obesity
School Violence
Stem Cells
Terrorist Attacks
U.S. Border Control
Video Games
World Energy Crisis

## Diseases and Disorders

ADHD
Alzheimer's Disease
Anorexia
Autism
Bipolar Disorders
Hepatitis

HPV
Meningitis
Phobias
Sexually Transmitted
    Diseases

## Drugs

Alcohol
Antidepressants
Club Drugs
Cocaine and Crack
Hallucinogens
Heroin
Inhalants

Marijuana
Methamphetamine
Nicotine and Tobacco
Performance-Enhancing
    Drugs
Prescription Drugs
Steroids

## Energy and the Environment

Biofuels
Deforestation
Hydrogen Power

Solar Power
Wind Power

*For a complete list of titles please visit www.referencepointpress.com.

COMPACT *Research*

# Fossil Fuels

by Lauri S. Friedman

## Energy and the Environment

ReferencePoint Press®

San Diego, CA

© 2010 ReferencePoint Press, Inc.

**For more information, contact:**
ReferencePoint Press, Inc.
PO Box 27779
San Diego, CA 92198
www. ReferencePointPress.com

Picture credits:
Cover: iStockphoto.com
Maury Aaseng: 32–35, 48–51, 64–66, 78–81
AP Images: 13
iStockphoto.com: 11

LIBRARY OF CONGRESS CATALOGING-IN-PUBLICATION DATA

Friedman, Lauri S.
    Fossil fuels / by Lauri S. Friedman.
        p. cm.—(Compact research series)
    Includes bibliographical references and index.
    ISBN-13: 978-1-60152-079-1 (hardback)
    ISBN-10: 1-60152-079-4 (hardback)
    1. Fossil fuels—Juvenile literature. I. Title.
    TP318.3.F75    2009
    333.8'2—dc22
                                                        2009003498

# Contents

# Foreword

**❝Where is the knowledge we have lost in information?❞**

—T.S. Eliot, "The Rock."

A s modern civilization continues to evolve, its ability to create, store, distribute, and access information expands exponentially. The explosion of information from all media continues to increase at a phenomenal rate. By 2020 some experts predict the worldwide information base will double every 73 days. While access to diverse sources of information and perspectives is paramount to any democratic society, information alone cannot help people gain knowledge and understanding. Information must be organized and presented clearly and succinctly in order to be understood. The challenge in the digital age becomes not the creation of information, but how best to sort, organize, enhance, and present information.

ReferencePoint Press developed the *Compact Research* series with this challenge of the information age in mind. More than any other subject area today, researching current issues can yield vast, diverse, and unqualified information that can be intimidating and overwhelming for even the most advanced and motivated researcher. The *Compact Research* series offers a compact, relevant, intelligent, and conveniently organized collection of information covering a variety of current topics ranging from illegal immigration and deforestation to diseases such as anorexia and meningitis.

The series focuses on three types of information: objective single-author narratives, opinion-based primary source quotations, and facts and statistics. The clearly written objective narratives provide context and reliable background information. Primary source quotes are carefully selected and cited, exposing the reader to differing points of view. And facts and statistics sections aid the reader in evaluating perspectives. Presenting these key types of information creates a richer, more balanced learning experience.

For better understanding and convenience, the series enhances information by organizing it into narrower topics and adding design features that make it easy for a reader to identify desired content. For example, in *Compact Research: Illegal Immigration*, a chapter covering the economic impact of illegal immigration has an objective narrative explaining the various ways the economy is impacted, a balanced section of numerous primary source quotes on the topic, followed by facts and full-color illustrations to encourage evaluation of contrasting perspectives.

The ancient Roman philosopher Lucius Annaeus Seneca wrote, "It is quality rather than quantity that matters." More than just a collection of content, the *Compact Research* series is simply committed to creating, finding, organizing, and presenting the most relevant and appropriate amount of information on a current topic in a user-friendly style that invites, intrigues, and fosters understanding.

# Fossil Fuels at a Glance

## Fossil Fuels and the Obama Energy Agenda

In February 2009, President Barack Obama signed the American Recovery and Reinvestment Act, a $787 billion economic stimulus bill that includes $3.4 billion for carbon capture and clean fossil fuels technology. Additionally, the Obama administration's "New Energy for America" plan sets out long-term energy goals such as ensuring that 25 percent of America's electricity comes from renewable sources by 2025 and investing $150 billion over 10 years to stimulate private clean energy projects. The how, what, and when of such spending has prompted considerable debate.

## World Oil Consumption

Oil is currently consumed around the globe at a rate of more than 80 million barrels per day.

## U.S. Oil Consumption

The United States is the largest consumer of oil in the world, consuming about 20 million barrels of oil per day—nearly 25 percent of the global daily total.

## Projected World Oil Supply

At current consumption rates, the world's supply of oil is expected to last about 40 to 43 years.

## Projected World Natural Gas Supply

At current consumption rates, the world's supply of natural gas is expected to last between 65 and 167 years.

## Projected World Coal Supply

At current consumption rates, the world's supply of coal is expected to last between 225 and 417 years.

## Proven Oil Reserves

The amount of oil that has been proved to exist is continually growing. In 1926 proven oil reserves were 4.5 billion barrels and currently stand at 1.3 trillion barrels.

## A Growing Demand for Energy

World energy demand is expected to increase by 45 percent between now and 2030—an average rate of increase of 1.6 percent per year.

## Fossil Fuels and Climate Change

In 2007 the Intergovernmental Panel on Climate Change (IPCC) concluded with 90 percent certainty that the burning of fossil fuels is contributing to climate change. That same year, 100 reputable scientists countered the IPCC's conclusions, arguing that new research shows otherwise.

## U.S. and Foreign Oil

The United States imports the most oil of any country in the world, bringing in 13.5 million barrels each day from foreign sources. Almost 64 percent of total U.S. daily consumption comes from foreign sources.

## Projected U.S. Oil Imports

The Energy Information Administration predicts that by 2017, the United States will be importing approximately 68 percent of its oil from foreign sources. By 2027 it will be importing 70 percent.

## Gas Prices

The national average price of a gallon (3.8L) of unleaded self-serve regular gasoline set a record high of $4.11 on July 17, 2008.

# Overview

66Unless we massively change our behavior, and reduce our consumption of energy to 10 or 20 percent of what it is at present, then there is no possibility of sustaining the sort of lives that we know.99

—George Monbiot, columnist for the *Guardian* newspaper and author of *Heat: How to Stop the Planet Burning*.

66This is a new oil age, not the end of oil as we know it.99

—Leonardo Maugeri, author of *The Age of Oil: The Mythology, History, and Future of the World's Most Controversial Resource*.

In 1859 the world was changed forever when a man named Edwin L. Drake struck oil in the first commercially successful well. With this singular act, the modern petroleum industry in the United States was born. As a result of this and similar discoveries, human civilization made progress in astonishing leaps and bounds, as fossil fuels unlocked a world of development, discovery, invention, travel, communication, and cooperation between nations.

Yet since this boom, fossil fuels have had an increasingly dark cloud cast over their use. Fossil fuel use is complicated by four main issues: supply, environmental impact, security, and necessity.

## Are We Running Out of Fossil Fuels?

Whether the world is running out of fossil fuels is a key concern associated with their use. All fossil fuels—oil, natural gas, coal, and other petroleum derivatives—were created millions of years ago, when the remains of organisms became buried under layers of mud and rock, where they were exposed to high levels of heat and pressure. Although fossil fuels only began to be used in the 1700s, humans have burned them so rapidly since then that it is feared we are going through the finite—or limited—supply too quickly.

The end of the fossil fuel era was first posited in 1956 by a geoscientist named Marion King Hubbert, who predicted that the supply of oil and other fossil fuels would hit a peak before they began to decline. As the theory goes, oil that is extracted before the peak hits is easiest to get out. But when about half the oil from an oil field has been removed, it gets harder and more expensive to get the remaining amount out. The last third to

*Forests had to be cleared to install this natural gas pipeline in Canada. At current consumption rates, the world's supply of natural gas is expected to last between 65 and 167 years.*

quarter is so expensive and difficult, it is not even worth extracting. This fact, coupled with the knowledge that fossil fuels take millions of years to replenish themselves, has caused many people to worry that humanity's continued reliance on them is a recipe for disaster. As environmental writer Jim Lydecker has said, "The slide down peak oil is unstoppable."[1] So, too, it is feared, is humanity's way of life if it does not begin to replace fossil fuels with renewable resources.

> " Fossil fuel use is complicated by four main issues: supply, environmental impact, security, and necessity. "

Yet many reject the conventional wisdom that fossil fuels will soon run out. For one, no one knows exactly how much fossil fuel the Earth holds. New reserves of it are found every year, and the world currently has more barrels of oil in its proven reserves—the amount we know for sure exists and is readily extractable—than at any other point in history. Journalist Vasko Kohlmayer has predicted that by 2015, these reserves could increase by as much as 25 percent. Secondly, new technologies are continually helping extract oil from new places—miles beneath the ocean, for example, or from the increasingly melting Arctic—or even process it from previously unknown sources, such as tar sands and shale rock.

## Does Fossil Fuel Use Threaten the Environment?

If the debate over fossil fuels were simply limited to their supply, it perhaps might cause less controversy. But even if the Earth holds plenty of fossil fuels, the impact of their use on the environment would remain a controversial issue. The burning of fossil fuels releases large amounts of greenhouse gases, particularly carbon dioxide ($CO_2$), into the Earth's atmosphere. Increased amounts of $CO_2$ have been linked to climate change, which, if left unchecked, is expected to have devastating effects on sea levels, weather patterns, food and water supplies, and the spread of disease. Scientists and politicians are increasingly blaming humanity's addiction to fossil fuels for global warming and have stressed the importance of finding alternative energy sources.

But global warming is only one of the environmental debates relating to fossil fuels. Their use has also been connected to air and water pollu-

*Kayford Mountain, in West Virginia, has been destroyed so that coal companies can mine the coal inside. More than 460 mountains—an area that together equals the state of Delaware—have been depleted or destroyed by coal mining in the United States.*

tion, which in turn can cause cancer and other illnesses. When fossil fuels are transported around the globe, there are sometimes accidents that result in catastrophic oil spills that threaten both wildlife and their habitat. Finally, the extraction of coal, natural gas, and oil from the earth causes the pollution of groundwater supplies and the destruction of mountains and forests (which are dynamited or cut down to access the fossil fuels within). Yet in this area, too, technology is lessening some of the concerns people have about the environmental impact of fossil fuel use. Take Alaska's Arctic National Wildlife Refuge (ANWR), which has been a hot spot of controversy for years. The refuge is located in about 1.5 million acres (607,028ha) of pristine wilderness, an untouched, wild world that is home to hundreds of species of animals. Environmentalists believe the pristine wilderness should be protected from the environmental degradation that would be brought on by oil excavation. Yet those who want to drill in ANWR claim the operation will have minimal impact on nature. The environment would be adequately protected, they argue, if they use state-of-the art drilling equipment that employs satellite imaging to pinpoint exactly where drilling is needed, which minimizes harm to surrounding wildlife and habitat. Other technology, such as trucks with huge tires called rolligons, can minimize the impact of the vehicles on the region's delicate landscape. "Trying to explain to a tie-dyed-in-the-wool 'green' environmentalist that drilling for oil in ANWR won't harm the environment is like trying to convince a 5-year-old that there is no Santa Claus," says Peyton Knight, analyst for the National Center for Public Policy Research. "The evidence may be clear, but he just won't believe it."[2] Whether drilling in ANWR can truly be an environmentally friendly endeavor is just one of the environmental controversies surrounding fossil fuel use.

> "Scientists and politicians are increasingly blaming humanity's addiction to fossil fuels for global warming and have stressed the importance of finding alternative energy sources."

## How Does Fossil Fuel Use Affect National Security?

In addition to supply and the environment, a third concern of fossil fuel use is whether it compromises America's national security. The United States is currently the largest consumer of oil in the world, consuming about 20 million barrels of oil per day. Most of that—about 64 percent—is imported from foreign countries. According to the Energy Information Administration, by 2017 the United States will be importing approximately 68 percent of its oil from foreign sources. As such, it will be—and in some opinions, already is—overwhelmingly dependent on other countries for its oil. This subjects the United States to the whims of other nations. Many of the world's oil-exporting countries also happen to be unstable or unfriendly to the United States. Notes analyst Ariel Cohen, "This social and political instability characterizes all of the major oil provinces: the Middle East, Venezuela, and Africa."[3]

Being so reliant on unfriendly and unstable countries for a key resource naturally raises concerns among those charged with America's safety and security. These concerns arose during the oil embargo of 1973, in which oil-exporting nations placed a ban on oil sales to the United States to punish it for its support of Israel in the Arab-Israeli War of that year. The price of gasoline quadrupled overnight, and oil-rationing resulted in mammoth lines for gas and a general sense of panic that lasted until the embargo was lifted in 1974.

Furthermore, America's heavy foreign fossil fuel consumption has been blamed for keeping the nation engaged in protracted, bloody, expensive "resource wars" and for making it and its allies the targets of terrorism. Indeed, when the United States gets involved in international conflicts to ensure its access to cheap oil (as some claim it has done in Iraq), it garners the resentment, even hatred, of people such as al Qaeda leader Osama bin Laden, who linked the terrorist attacks of September 11, 2001, to America's pursuit of oil. Bin Laden and other terrorists have justified their attacks as punishment for what they view as America's undying quest for cheap

> **Fossil fuels continue to be used despite all the issues surrounding them because no other energy source has yet been able to match their power, availability, or cost.**

fossil fuels. This is perhaps why a 2006 *Foreign Policy* poll of more than 100 foreign policy experts revealed that 82 percent of them believe that ending America's dependence on foreign oil should be the United States' single most pressing priority for national security—more pressing even than fighting terrorism.

As a result of the multiple issues surrounding fossil fuel use, the U.S. government has made a commitment to reducing the amount of oil imported from dangerous foreign sources. In 2008, for example, the U.S. Energy Information Administration projected that oil imports will actually drop to around 40 percent as the United States increasingly turns to homegrown renewable sources of energy. Whether this will be achievable, however, remains to be seen.

## Can Alternative Energy Sources Replace Fossil Fuels?

The most commonly discussed alternatives to fossil fuels are nuclear power and renewable resources such as wind, solar, hydropower, biofuels, and hydrogen. Each of these energy sources has advantages and drawbacks, and it is likely that as the United States turns away from fossil fuels, these alternatives will be used in concert to offer a multifaceted approach to energy. Thus far, none of them alone has proven powerful enough, cost-effective enough, or safe enough to do the job on its own.

Fossil fuels continue to be used despite all the issues surrounding their use because no other energy source has yet been able to match their power, availability, or cost. Humanity's dependence on fossil fuels is noted by both supporters and opponents of their use. David B. Sandalow, energy analyst for the Brookings Institution, has put the problem in the following way: "If I'm thirsty and don't feel like a glass of water, I can have soda or orange juice. If I'm hungry and don't feel like eating a hamburger, I can have a hot dog or pasta. But if I want to travel any significant distance in the world today and don't want to use petroleum, I'm basically out of luck."[4]

## A World Without Fossil Fuels

Alternative sources of energy have been difficult to find in part because fossil fuels power so much. When most people think of how fossil fuels are used, they immediately think of the gas they burn to run their car and the electricity they use to light their homes. Yet fossil fuels power more than just transportation and electricity. They are the key ingredients of other important industries that Americans rely on to get through their everyday lives.

When imagining a world without fossil fuels, begin with food. When most Americans look down at their dinner plate each evening, they see something delicious: baked macaroni and cheese, perhaps, or grilled chicken and salad. What most *do not* see are the barrels of oil it took to grow, feed, chill, and transport those ingredients to their kitchens, causing their meals to be, in the words of author Michael Pollen, "drenched in fossil fuel."[5]

Oil began to play a critical role in the food industry in the middle of the twentieth century, when fossil fuel–derived fertilizers, pesticides, herbicides, and irrigation began being used to produce larger quantities of food for mass consumption. These technologies helped crops to grow bigger and more densely and to better resist pests and weeds. They also helped transport water to otherwise dry places where animals and crops could be raised. While each of these advances significantly increased the amount and hardiness of food that is able to be produced, each is fueled by, or derived entirely from, fossil fuels.

## Food and Fossil Fuels

Dale Allen Pfeiffer, author of *Eating Fossil Fuels: Oil, Food and the Coming Crisis in Agriculture*, estimates that it takes 400 gallons (1,514L) of oil a year to provide food for each American. This oil is consumed in the long chain that is the commercial food industry. It is used to make fertilizers and operate harvesting and other farm-related machinery. It powers the irrigation systems that transport water to crops grown in dry yet sunny places such as California and Arizona. It is used to make the plastic containers in which most food is packaged and to power the refrigerators in which food is stored. Finally, it is used to transport food to distribution centers and supermarkets all around the country. This last step is more resource intensive and expensive than ever—according to the Environmental Defense Fund, the average meal in 2008 traveled between 1,500 and 2,500 miles (2,414 and 4,023 km) to get from the farm to the dinner table.

> " The average meal in 2008 traveled between 1,500 and 2,500 miles (2,414 and 4,023km) to get from the farm to the dinner table. "

Pollen, author of *The Omnivore's Dilemma*, breaks down the food–fossil fuel link even further. Pollen estimates that it takes about 7 to 10 calories of fossil fuel energy to make 1 calorie of food energy. In other words, between 4,900 and 7,000 calories of fossil fuel energy go into creating

> " *All plastics—from toys, to packaging materials, to office equipment, to iPods, to credit cards, to computers, even to the plastic parts of cars that are then powered by fossil fuels—are derived in some way from oil.* "

the approximately 700-calorie dinner most Americans eat each evening. Pollen realized the inefficiency of this process when he stopped to consider that his dinner included imported "asparagus traveling in a 747 from Argentina; blackberries trucked up from Mexico; [and] a salad chilled to thirty-six degrees from the moment it was picked in Arizona."[6] Each of these activities are the reason the food industry is responsible for burning nearly a fifth of all the petroleum consumed in the United States each year. Indeed, when the food industry is examined through the lens of fossil fuel use, it becomes easy to agree with Pfeiffer, who has said, "In a very real sense, we are literally eating fossil fuels."[7] Eating seasonally available, locally produced, organic food is one way that both Pollen and Pfeiffer say people can reduce the amount of fossil fuels that are burned to produce each meal.

## Oil and Plastic

Another item that inherently depends on oil is plastic. Looking at a water bottle or CD case, one might never guess that it was born from the black, slippery crude that is extracted hundreds of feet below the surface of the Earth. But all plastics—from toys, to packaging materials, to office equipment, to iPods, to credit cards, to computers, even to the plastic parts of cars that are then powered by fossil fuels—are derived in some way from oil.

Plastic comes from compounds found in oil called hydrocarbons. These hydrocarbons are extracted from oil when it is heated to more than 750°F (399°C), or until they can be separated out into polymers, or long chains of molecules. These chains exist in the form of pellets, which are molded into a specific shape at a factory. Their use is nearly endless—and very resource intensive.

According to reporter Simon Usborne, "For every barrel of oil that goes into making plastic, another is required to fuel the process."[8] As a result, the production of plastics accounts for 7 million barrels of petroleum every day—or 8 percent of the total amount of oil consumed around the world every day. Those such as Richard Girard, a researcher at the Polaris Institute, find a great irony in the fact that bottled water, which is frequently billed as an environmentally benign product, is packaged in material that is made of fossil fuels. Writes Girard, "The intimate connections between the bottled water industry and the dirty oil, petrochemical and plastic industries fundamentally contradict the attempts by the water companies to paint their products as healthy and clean."[9]

Because plastic products suck up so much oil, recycling them is an important part of conserving this fossil fuel. The Environmental Protection Agency (EPA) estimates that products made from recycled materials use a third less energy than products made from brand-new plastic. Put another way, 1 ton (0.9 metric ton) of recycled plastic can save an estimated 685 gallons (2,593L) of oil. The EPA and other environmental organizations recommend recycling and alternative methods of packaging—such as using reusable canvas bags at the grocery store rather than plastic ones—to cut down on the amount of plastic we consume.

> " **Nearly every facet of modern American life is in some way connected to fossil fuels.** "

## Oil Is Woven into Our Way of Life

Food and plastic are two of the largest industries that feature petroleum-based products, but the list does not stop there. Oil is also a key ingredient in the manufacturing of medicines, pharmaceuticals, and vitamins. For example, acetylsalicylic acid, the active ingredient in many over-the-counter pain relievers, is derived from petroleum-based chemicals, called petrochemicals. Medical equipment, from basic first-aid tools such as bandages and nonstick pads to larger medical machinery, also have their origins in petrochemicals.

Oil-based products also keep us comfortable and our homes looking nice—carpets, couches, curtains, certain types of clothing fabric, even the paint on most of our walls is derived in some part from petroleum. Oil even plays a role in entertaining us—cassette tapes, CDs, records, and DVDs are all made from petroleum-based products.

Wax is another petroleum product, and from it spring candles, milk and juice cartons, garbage bags, even glossy, edible, food coatings that make apples and cucumbers appear shiny. Oil-based food additives are a common ingredient in canned goods, helping them stay fresher longer. Car tires and sneakers, pen ink and camera film, rope and makeup, hair dye and Styrofoam—each is made at least in part from fossil fuels. It is no wonder, then, that writer Jim Lydecker has unequivocally declared, "No substance is more interwoven into life as oil."[10]

> " Alternatives to fossil fuels . . . will need to be as multifaceted and complex as fossil fuel use currently is. "

Nearly every facet of modern American life is in some way connected to fossil fuels. As such, oil consumption in these and other industries must be considered when debating the future of fossil fuels, and replacements are obviously difficult to find. Nuclear power may be able to provide larger amounts of cheap, carbon-free electricity, but it is unlikely to be able to be used to power cars and trucks. In the same way, relying more on wind and solar power might be useful to reduce the amount of coal burned to create electricity, but will not help find an alternative to plastic packaging. Alternatives to fossil fuels, in other words, will need to be as multifaceted and complex as fossil fuels currently are. The coming years and decades will reveal much about the future of fossil fuels—whether we are in fact running out of them, whether their use is in fact causing dangerous climate change, and whether alternative energy sources can be found to effectively power, feed, and otherwise support the billions of people on Earth.

# Is the World Running Out of Fossil Fuels?

> **The amount of oil in the ground simply doesn't grow.**
>
> —Julian Darley, founder and director of the Post Carbon Institute and Global Public Media.

> **The notion that this planet is running out of oil is one of the great misnomers of our age.**
>
> Vasko Kohlmayer, columnist and contributor to the *American Thinker*, the *Baltimore Sun*, and other publications.

Debates surrounding fossil fuels begin with the fact that they are a nonrenewable, or finite, resource. Fossil fuels are called "nonrenewable" because they take millions of years to form and are used up faster than that. All fossil fuels—oil, natural gas, coal, and other petroleum outputs—were created when the remains of organisms became buried in the earth under layers of mud, sediment, and rock. Over time, high levels of heat and pressure triggered chemical reactions that turned the organic matter into various forms of fossil fuel. Many argue that the world needs to find a new energy source in preparation for the nearing day when oil wells dry up. But is the world actually running out of fossil fuels?

The end of oil was first predicted in 1956 by scientist Marion King Hubbert in a theory that became known as "Hubbert's Peak." The theory states that oil supplies will reach a high point—a peak—and then begin a downward spiral until they are used up or it becomes technically impossible or financially infeasible to extract them from the ground. Colin Campbell, head of the Oil Depletion Analysis Centre in London, explains peak oil theory in the following way: "It's quite a simple theory. . . . The glass starts full and ends empty and the faster you drink it the quicker it's gone."[11] Hubbert predicted that American oil supplies would peak in 1970, and that the global oil supply would peak in 1999 or 2000. He was close to the mark about U.S. oil production, which ended up peaking in 1974.

It is hard to predict how much fossil fuel is still in the ground and how long the remaining supply will last. It depends on how fast humans use the fuel and what technologies will be developed to yield new sources. The *Oil & Gas Journal*, which tends to publish optimistic reserve estimates, claims that at current consumption rates, the world's supply of oil will last another 43 years, natural gas another 167 years, and coal another 417 years. Estimates from more conservative sources have oil running out in about 40 years, natural gas in 65 years, and coal in 225 years or less.

> It is hard to predict how much fossil fuel is still in the ground and how long the remaining supply will last.

No matter what the exact date, though, many are sure this finite resource will one day become exhausted. Already, some of the world's most productive oil fields have slowed their output. The date Hubbert predicted for peak oil to hit has come and gone, and many scientists say peak oil is either already upon us, or it will hit between 2005 and 2010 and not later than 2020. Even some oil executives have admitted it is only a matter of time before all of the oil that is cheap and easy to get dries up. Journalist Joseph Romm reports that in 2008 the chief executive officer of Royal Dutch/Shell said easy-to-access oil and gas will disappear in 2015. "It used to be unheard of for oil executives to talk about limits to oil production," writes Romm. "Now it happens all the time."[12]

Global polls show that citizens of almost every nation on Earth are concerned about dwindling supplies of fossil fuels. A whopping 70 percent of citizens from 15 countries said in a 2008 poll that they believe oil supplies have already peaked. Further adding to the worry is exponential growth in developing nations like China and India, which threaten to rip through the global supply at a ferocious rate. As columnist Jim Lydecker writes: "It's a finite resource, a geological gift of nature, half of which we've run through in less than 150 years. You only have to look as far as the mature, collapsing fields [of] the North Sea, Mexico's Cantarell, Alaska's North Slope, Russia's Caspian and various Middle Eastern countries to know we are in deep trouble."[13]

## New Technology Yields More Oil

Yet technological developments and environmental change are revealing new sources of fossil fuels every year, producing figures that cast doubt on the conventionally accepted theory of peak oil. Especially as the price of oil rises, it is worth explorers' while to search for oil in places where it was previously too expensive to do so. This yields billions more barrels that stave off the end of oil, and even negate it, in some opinions. In fact, a 2008 report by the U.S. Geological Survey declared oil reserves to be at "an all-time high."[14]

Those who deny peak oil theory point out that with each passing year, the number of proven oil reserves grows. (Proven reserves means the amount of oil that is identified, affordable, and easy to extract). In 1882 there were only 95 million barrels of proven petroleum reserves. By 1926 so much additional oil had been discovered that the number of proven reserves had grown to 4.5 billion barrels, and to 10 billion barrels by 1932. In 1993 proven reserves had jumped to 999 billion, and currently stand at 1.3 trillion barrels. So even with more people using oil every year, the proven reserves keep growing. Says columnist Vasko Kohlmayer, "We can be virtually assured that two or three decades from now we will be talking about another 40 or 50 or more years worth of crude."[15]

> " Global polls show that citizens of almost every nation on Earth are concerned about dwindling supplies of fossil fuels. "

One reason the proven reserves keep expanding is because each year, new exploration techniques are perfected that allow drillers to find new fields. In 2007, for example, a large oil field that was estimated to hold 8 billion barrels was discovered off the coast of Brazil. Another reservoir nearby was discovered in 2008, this one expected to hold 30 billion barrels. In years past it was not cost-effective to make such discoveries. But with oil prices on the rise, such techniques become more affordable to use.

Secondly, technological advances—such as seismic instruments and drills that move horizontally—continue to improve excavators' ability to get oil out of places they were not able to in decades past. In the twentieth century, the average rate of oil recovery from a typical reservoir was 20 percent—meaning that excavators could get 20 percent of the oil out easily and cost-effectively. In the twenty-first century, however, that rate is almost 40 percent. In this way, technology has helped oil excavators find new wells and recover oil more efficiently from them.

> " **Technological developments and environmental change are revealing new sources of fossil fuels every year.** "

For all of these reasons, the world's proven reserves appear to grow each year. This is why some claim that predictions about oil supply will continue to increase even as consumption levels rise. Explains Kohlmayer, "In 1986 . . . it was estimated that the world's proved reserves would last 38 years. On that estimate we should only have 17 years worth of oil left. But because the figure in the 'proved reserves' column keeps getting larger, we now have more than 40 years."[16]

## Deepwater Drilling

Deepwater drilling is another technique that is helping excavators recover oil from previously inaccessible places. Using cutting-edge sonar technology and equipment that can cost more than $500 million, explorers are finding oil deeper in the ocean than ever before, increasing the number of proven reserves on Earth.

Deepwater drilling was used in 2006 to discover oil 5 miles (8km) beneath the surface of the Gulf of Mexico. To find the oil, a well was dug through 7,000 feet (2,134m) of water and more than 20,000 feet (6,096m) of seafloor. Oil was struck in a layer of rock that geologists estimate was formed between 24 and 65 million years ago. This underwater field is expected to yield between 3 and 15 billion barrels of crude oil, which could boost U.S. reserves by as much as 50 percent. Excavators believe new drills may be able to go as deep as 35,000 feet (10,668m) below sea level, helping them reach other promising deepwater locations off the coasts of Brazil, the United Kingdom, West Africa, and Southeast Asia.

> **For those seeking to maximize fossil fuel output, the melting Arctic is revealing itself as the next place to look.**

Deepwater drilling is not without controversy, however. Environmentalists claim that drilling techniques harm whales and other wildlife and release pollutants into the ocean. Plus it is fantastically expensive and time-consuming to extract such oil. But as the price of oil rises, expensive and risky drilling techniques like this become more profitable to pursue. Says Kohlmayer, "We can be reasonably certain that new exploration and advancing technologies will in coming years greatly add to the quantities of available oil."[17] As a result, he and other experts have even gone so far as to label oil not a renewable but an "infinite" resource.

## Climate Change to Yield More Oil

In an ironic twist, climate change—believed to be brought on by the burning of fossil fuels—is actually helping to reveal more of them. Melting of the polar ice caps, for example, is expected to make accessible billions of barrels of oil that have never before been identified. As the Earth's temperature rises, more of the frozen area north of the Arctic Circle melts and becomes exposed. In addition to scores of minerals and new trade routes, the melting of the area is expected to reveal completely untapped sources of fossil fuels.

A 2008 report by the U.S. Geological Survey estimated that the Arctic holds 90 billion barrels of oil, 1,670 trillion cubic feet (47 trillion cu. m) of natural gas (about 30 percent of all the undiscovered gas in the world), and 44 billion barrels of natural gas liquids—all of it as of yet undiscovered.

Some of these resources are believed to be concentrated in certain areas—a field in Russian waters, for example, is thought to contain enough natural gas to power the U.S. electrical grid alone for 6 years. Similarly, the area off the coast of Greenland is expected to be particularly rich in fossil fuels— retreating ice is revealing fields there that experts believe contain as many as 31 billion barrels of oil and natural gas.

> A growing chorus of voices argues that the debate over whether fossil fuels are running out is increasingly moot.

For this reason geologists who have explored the area have called it "the geographically largest unexplored prospective area for petroleum remaining on Earth."[18] Of course, retreating ice is believed to have more harmful consequences than benefits—all of that melting water is expected to raise sea levels, threaten coastal territory, and push global warming past a "tipping point" from which it may not be able to recover. But for those seeking to maximize fossil fuel output, the melting Arctic is revealing itself as the next place to look.

## Unconventional Sources: Tar Sands and Oil Shale

Not even factored into the world's proven reserves is oil that is extracted from more expensive and harder-to-reach places, also known as unconventional sources of oil. The two main unconventional sources from which it is possible to extract oil are tar sands and shale rock. Billions of barrels of oil are tied up in these sources, and there are pros and cons about releasing them.

Tar sands (also called oil sands) are actually made up of a substance called bitumen, which is a very thick and low-quality form of crude oil. To produce oil from tar sands, the bitumen must be strip-mined and heavily processed. The process of making crude oil from tar sands has been heavily criticized by environmental groups, which say its production alone uses more oil and produces more pollution than the oil from the sands is worth. A 2008 report by the Rand Corporation, sponsored by the National Commission on Energy Policy, found that producing oil from tar sands releases 10 to 30 percent more emissions than conventionally produced crude oil. Extracting oil from tar sands also requires a lot of water, another precious natural resource. Despite these environmental issues, the oil that could be yielded from tar sands could conceivably reach millions of barrels per day.

Oil shale is another unconventional fossil fuel source. Shale is a kind of rock from which a substance called kerogen can be extracted—after extensive processing, this substance can yield synthetic crude oil. According to the U.S. Department of Energy, the United States is home to 2 trillion barrels of the world's estimated 2.8 to 3.3 trillion barrels of oil shale. Much of this is located in Wyoming, Colorado, and Utah. This amount could meet America's oil needs at current consumption rates for 110 years. Says author Daniel Fine, a believer in the future of oil shale: "There is enough shale to sustain United States consumption of crude oil easily through 2120."[19]

But like the oil extracted from tar sands, recovering shale oil contaminates groundwater and produces toxic waste. It is also resource-intensive to make—one way of recovering shale oil, for example, consumes about 1 barrel of oil for every 6 produced. As the Natural Resources Defense Council, the Sierra Club, World Wildlife Fund, Greenpeace, the Rainforest Action Network, Friends of the Earth, and more than a dozen other environmental groups wrote in a letter to U.S. senators: "Production of [these] unconventional fuels . . . emit more than twice the global warming pollution per barrel as conventional oil at a time when we must be reducing our $CO_2$ emissions."[20]

## Peak or No Peak, Fossil Fuel Use Must End

A growing chorus of voices argues that the debate over whether fossil fuels are running out is increasingly moot. As climate change brought on by the burning of fossil fuels becomes more of a concern, people say it does not matter whether oil could last another 40 or 400 years—getting off of it immediately is what is best for the planet and its inhabitants. As Romm warns, "The growing threat of global warming requires deep reductions in national and global oil consumption starting now, peak or no peak."[21] In other words, greater fossil fuel supplies would not fix the other problems caused by their use, and it is within this context that future debates over fossil fuel use will likely occur.

# Is the World Running Out of Fossil Fuels?

66 **The choice is simple. Continue as we are, and wake up one morning to the sound of the wells sucking dry or implement policies that will at least mitigate the problems that lie ahead.** 99

—Oliver Dixon, "A World Without Oil," *Commercial Motor*, January 25, 2007.

Dixon is an automotive consultant and commentator and the host of the Road Transport blog.

66 **Contrary to the conventional wisdom, mankind's oil supplies are not getting depleted, but they keep continually expanding. . . . Earth's proved reserves could increase by as much as 25 percent by 2015.** 99

—Vasko Kohlmayer, "The Truth About Oil," *Front Page*, May 8, 2008. www.frontpagemag.com.

Kohlmayer is a journalist whose work has appeared in the *Baltimore Sun*, the *American Thinker*, and other publications.

" Here is the hard truth: Oil is running out. . . . Every oil company knows that. Every major automobile manufacturer knows that. Every politician who got a decent score on a scholastic aptitude test knows that. "

—Warren Brown, "News Flash: We're Running Out of Oil. Get Used to It," *Washington Post*, May 28, 2006, p. G02.

Brown writes a regular column about cars for the *Washington Post*.

" Over the decades, all attempts to evaluate our planet's oil endowment have proved too conservative. . . . This is a new oil age, not the end of oil as we know it. "

—Leonardo Maugeri, "What Lies Below?" *Newsweek*, December 4, 2006. www.newsweek.com.

Maugeri is the author of the book *The Age of Oil: The Mythology, History, and Future of the World's Most Controversial Resource.*

" Once peak oil sinks its claws into the Middle Eastern fields, the world of oil is going to shift dramatically. These two sources—oil sands and oil shale—may be part of the solution we're looking for. "

—Keith Kohl, "An Unconventional Solution," *Energy and Capital*, April 5, 2007. www.energyandcapital.com.

Kohl is the editor of *Energy and Capital*.

" Producing fuel in unconventional ways, such as from oil sands or coal, would significantly increase carbon emissions relative to conventional oil production. "

—Kate Galbraith, "The Costs of Unconventional Fossil Fuels," *New York Times*, October 8, 2008. www.nytimes.com.

Galbraith is an Austin-based journalist whose articles have appeared in the *New York Times*, *Slate.com*, AlterNet, and other media sources.

66 If shale is commercialized by 2012, we can, under production from Colorado alone, eliminate dependency on Middle East oil by 2020. 99

—Daniel Fine, "Oil Shale: Toward a Strategic Unconventional Fuels Supply Policy," Heritage Foundation, Lecture No. 1015, April 26, 2007. www.heritage.org.

Fine is coeditor of the book *Resource War in 3-D: Dependence, Diplomacy and Defense.*

66 The considerable economic, social and environmental drawbacks of CTL [coal-to-liquids], tar sands, and oil shale preclude them from being sound options for achieving greater energy independence. All three of these unconventional fuels afflict serious harm on the land, the water, the air, and on local communities. 99

—Friends Committee on National Legislation, "Oppose Environmentally Harmful Alternative Fuels Amendments to DOD Authorization Bill (Senate)," May 7, 2008. www.fcnl.org.

The Friends Committee on National Legislation is a coalition of groups that support peaceful solutions to America's problems.

# Facts and Illustrations

## Is the World Running Out of Fossil Fuels?

- A 2008 poll of **15,000 citizens** of 15 different countries and the Palestinian territories found:
  - **70 percent** believe oil supplies have already peaked
  - **22 percent** believe more oil will be found
  - In the United States **76 percent** said they believe oil is running out
  - The only nation where the majority of citizens said oil is not running out was Nigeria (where **53 percent** of the population believes enough new oil will be found)

- The world is estimated to hold more than **3 trillion barrels** of oil from shale—an amount more than twice the world's current crude oil reserves.

- The United States holds between **62 and 75 percent** of the world's supply of oil shale. The shale in Wyoming, Colorado, and Utah alone is expected eventually to be capable of producing between **3 and 5 million barrels** per day for more than 100 years.

- The United States holds about **27 percent** of the world's recoverable coal.

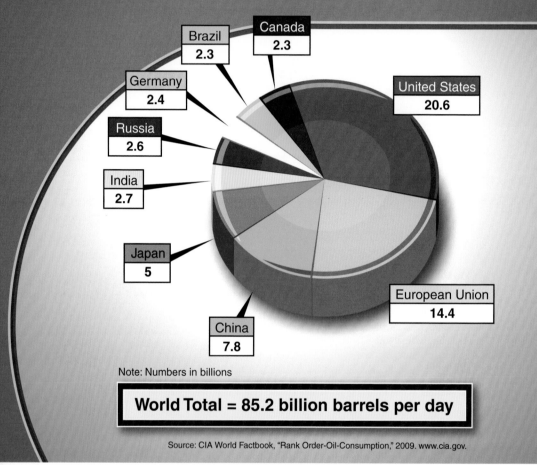

## Oil Consumption Around the World

Of all the oil consumed around the world each day, the United States is responsible for nearly 25 percent, consuming more than 20.6 billion barrels of oil per day.

| | |
|---|---|
| Brazil | 2.3 |
| Canada | 2.3 |
| Germany | 2.4 |
| Russia | 2.6 |
| India | 2.7 |
| Japan | 5 |
| China | 7.8 |
| United States | 20.6 |
| European Union | 14.4 |

Note: Numbers in billions

**World Total = 85.2 billion barrels per day**

Source: CIA World Factbook, "Rank Order-Oil-Consumption," 2009. www.cia.gov.

- According to the London-based Oil Depletion Analysis Centre:
  - Easy-to-reach oil **peaked in 2005**.
  - Global oil production will peak by the year **2011**, even when one factors in heavy oil, deep sea reserves, polar regions and liquid taken from gas.

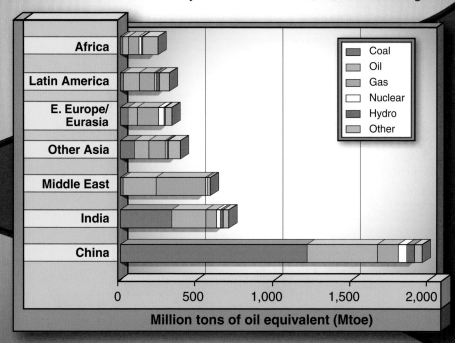

# Developing Nations' Energy Needs
## (2030 Estimates)

In coming years and decades, explosive growth in developing nations is expected to threaten the global supply of fossil fuels. China alone is expected to need enormous amounts of energy by 2030, and much of it is likely to come from coal, oil, and natural gas.

**Legend:**
- Coal
- Oil
- Gas
- Nuclear
- Hydro
- Other

Categories (top to bottom): Africa, Latin America, E. Europe/Eurasia, Other Asia, Middle East, India, China

X-axis: 0, 500, 1,000, 1,500, 2,000

**Million tons of oil equivalent (Mtoe)**

Source: World Energy Outlook, "Incremental Primary Energy Demand in the Reference Scenario, 2006–2030," 2008.

- According to the World Energy Outlook (published by the International Energy Agency):
  - World energy demand is expected to increase by **45 percent** between now and 2030—an average rate of increase of 1.6 percent per year.
  - China accounts for **43 percent** of the growth in global oil demand.
  - The Middle East accounts for **20 percent** of the growth in global oil demand.
  - Asian nations account for most of the rest.

# The Many Uses of Fossil Fuels

Nearly every facet of modern American life is in some way connected to fossil fuels. Here are just a few of the household items that are derived from them.

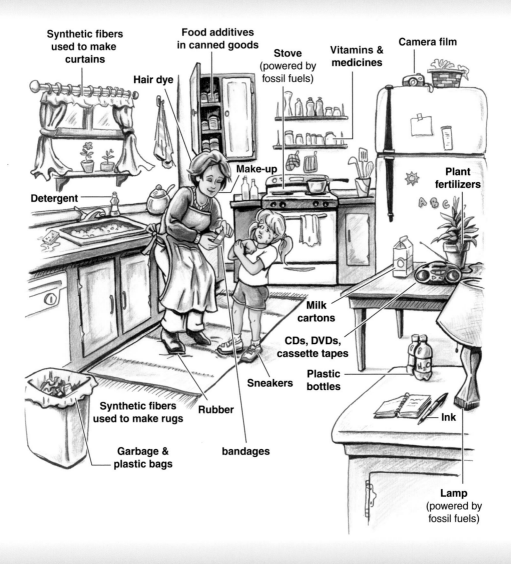

Synthetic fibers used to make curtains

Food additives in canned goods

Stove (powered by fossil fuels)

Vitamins & medicines

Camera film

Hair dye

Make-up

Plant fertilizers

Detergent

Milk cartons

CDs, DVDs, cassette tapes

Sneakers

Plastic bottles

Ink

Synthetic fibers used to make rugs

Rubber

Garbage & plastic bags

bandages

Lamp (powered by fossil fuels)

Source: The Paleontological Research Institution, "Oil and Everyday Life," 2009. www.priweb.org.

# Worldwide Oil Reserves

Saudi Arabia, Canada, Iraq, and Iran have the largest proven oil reserves in the world.

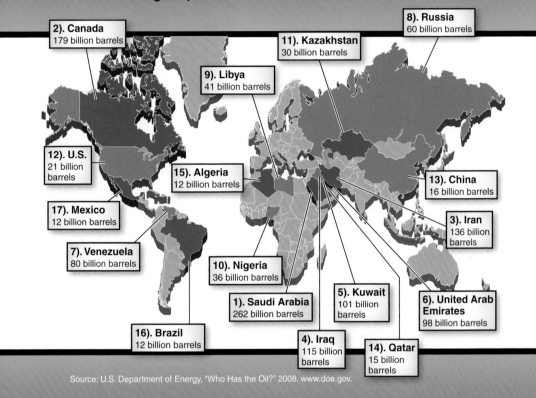

**2). Canada** 179 billion barrels

**8). Russia** 60 billion barrels

**11). Kazakhstan** 30 billion barrels

**9). Libya** 41 billion barrels

**12). U.S.** 21 billion barrels

**15). Algeria** 12 billion barrels

**13). China** 16 billion barrels

**17). Mexico** 12 billion barrels

**3). Iran** 136 billion barrels

**7). Venezuela** 80 billion barrels

**10). Nigeria** 36 billion barrels

**5). Kuwait** 101 billion barrels

**6). United Arab Emirates** 98 billion barrels

**1). Saudi Arabia** 262 billion barrels

**16). Brazil** 12 billion barrels

**4). Iraq** 115 billion barrels

**14). Qatar** 15 billion barrels

Source: U.S. Department of Energy, "Who Has the Oil?" 2008. www.doe.gov.

- The price of oil has **fluctuated** for many decades. According to the Energy Information Administration:
  - In 1978, a barrel of oil cost **$13.38**
  - In 1991, a barrel of oil cost **$24.06**
  - In 1998, a barrel of oil cost **$10.72**
  - In 2000, a barrel of oil cost **$27.14**
  - In 2005, a barrel of oil cost **$50.89**
  - In 2008, a barrel of oil cost **$133.60**
  - In 2009, a barrel of oil cost **$41.31**

# Does Fossil Fuel Use Threaten the Environment?

> 66'Clean coal' is like a healthy cigarette—it doesn't exist.99
>
> —Blan Holman, attorney with the Southern Environmental Law Center, Charleston, South Carolina.

> 66Maybe we should all take a deep breath of $CO_2$ and calm down.99
>
> —Mark Steyn, Canadian columnist and political commentator.

Along with national security and supply, environmental damage is increasingly cited as a main reason why fossil fuel use has become problematic. Whether and to what extent fossil fuel use has contributed to environmental damage, however, is a complicated matter.

## Does Fossil Fuel Use Cause Global Warming?

The most dangerous by-product of fossil fuel use is the greenhouse gas carbon dioxide ($CO_2$), which is believed to be responsible for global warming. $CO_2$ collects in the Earth's atmosphere, trapping heat and causing the planet to warm. Some amount of warming is natural and even necessary for life, but it is believed that too much $CO_2$ in the atmosphere causes the Earth's average temperature to rise unnaturally. Warming could cause melting ice caps to dump tons of water into the sea, raising levels by several inches or feet. In turn, rising seas threaten to drown low-lying islands, erode coastal property, and make the seas uninhabitable for many species of marine life. Global warming is believed to trigger an increase in severe weather such as hurricanes, droughts, tornadoes, and floods. It is also expected to help spread disease and threaten the growth of food crops.

Whether the burning of fossil fuels actually causes global warming has been a subject of debate for decades, and the debate has not cooled even as scientists learn more about the ways in which human activities affect the climate. As of 2009 a growing chorus of serious and reputable voices in the scientific and political communities had officially linked fossil fuel use with climate change. Most notably, this was the conclusion of a major international report published by the Intergovernmental Panel on Climate Change (IPCC) in 2007. The UN–backed report, which was written by hundreds of scientists from 113 countries, concluded with 90 percent certainty that humanity's reliance on oil, coal, and natural gas is to blame for global warming. Wrote the authors: "Human influences have: *very likely* contributed to sea level rise during the latter half of the 20th century; *likely* contributed to changes in wind patterns, affecting extra-tropical storm tracks and temperature patterns; [and] *likely* increased temperatures of extreme hot nights, cold nights and cold days."[22]

> The UN-backed report, which was written by hundreds of scientists from 113 countries, concluded with 90 percent certainty that humanity's reliance on oil, coal, and natural gas is to blame for global warming.

The authors predicted that these activities will, sometime this century, cause the world's temperature to rise so much that it will result in a catastrophic and irreversible rise in sea levels and species extinctions. The IPCC and similar reports published by the multinational Arctic Climate Impact Assessment, the Climate Trust, NASA's Goddard Institute for Space Studies, and others led president-elect Barack Obama in 2008 to declare, "The science is beyond dispute and the facts are clear." As he vowed to make reducing $CO_2$ emissions and investing in new energy-saving technologies a top priority of his presidency, he said, "Now is the time to confront this challenge once and for all. Delay is no longer an option. Denial is no longer an acceptable response."[23]

## Other Explanations for Climate Change

Yet many people doubt the claim that fossil fuel use has anything to do with climate change. They argue that fossil records show the planet has endured warming periods at other points in Earth's history, centuries before human industrial activity ever began. Some suggest that the climate naturally experiences shifts in temperature every 1,500 years, and as such the globe is right on schedule for a warming event. Others explain contemporary warming not as the result of greenhouse gas emissions but rather due to volcanoes, sunspots, geological shifts, and other natural causes.

If this is true, then it is argued that curbing fossil fuel use would needlessly set off a chain reaction that would hurt the economy and the American way of life. Hudson Institute scholar Dennis T. Avery is among many who wonder "whether we will frighten ourselves into extinction over a planetary warming that has totaled 0.2 degrees since 1940—right on the 1,500-year cycle's schedule."[24] In December 2007 a group of 100 reputable geologists, physicists, meteorologists, and other scientists echoed Avery's concerns in a letter they wrote to the UN secretary-general in which they disagreed with the IPCC's conclusions on climate change. "In stark contrast to the often repeated assertion that the science of climate change is 'settled,'" wrote the scientists, "significant new peer-reviewed research has cast even more doubt on the hypothesis of dangerous human-caused global warming."[25]

> Some suggest that the climate naturally experiences shifts in temperature every 1,500 years, and as such the globe is right on schedule for a warming event.

Several global polls reveal similar skepticism about the conventional wisdom that the burning of fossil fuels is causing climate change. A 2008 survey of some of Canada's most accomplished Earth scientists and engineers, for example, revealed that only about a quarter of them (26 percent) attribute global warming to human activity. Although 99 percent of those polled believe the climate is changing, 27 percent believe such warming is natural.

Suspicion of the fossil fuel–climate change link comes from other countries, too. In 2008 the results of an Ipsos MORI poll revealed that 60 percent of Britons said that scientific experts still question whether humans are contributing to climate change, while 40 percent said they sometimes think climate change might not be as bad as people say. In the United States a 2008 poll conducted by the Pew Research Center found that even though 71 percent of Americans believe the Earth is warming, just 47 percent say it is due to the burning of fossil fuels. Clearly, the debate over whether fossil fuel use is contributing to climate change is far from over.

## The Environmental Impact of Coal

Another fossil fuel frequently takes center stage in discussions of whether fossil fuels are bad for the environment: coal. Coal is a staple of America's energy program, providing 22 percent of its total energy. However, its use raises several environmental concerns.

While coal was once viewed as a very dirty energy source, coal advocates say this fossil fuel has gotten increasingly cleaner and more efficient. According to the American Coalition for Clean Coal Electricity, since 1970, dangerous pollutants from coal-fired power plants have been reduced between 70 and 95 percent, even as the nation has burned 3 times as much of it. Furthermore, the energy that comes from coal is important to America's security because it can be made at home. In fact, there is more coal in the United States than there is oil in the entire Middle East—the United States is believed to have about 27 percent of the world's total supply, which is expected to last 250 years or more.

In addition, coal is an important part of the U.S. economy, as it provides more than 50 percent of the nation's electricity needs and provides jobs for thousands of people. As columnist Paul Driessen has put it, "Coal's reliable, affordable electricity creates millions of high-paying jobs, and thus provides health insurance, rent and mortgage money, nutrition, clothing and retirement benefits for countless families."[26]

But coal use contributes significantly to air pollution and other environmental problems. The burning of coal also produces large amounts of mercury, which end up in the world's oceans and seas and ultimately in the food supply. Finally, coal-fired plants produce a lot of $CO_2$, the main gas linked to climate change. According to the U.S. Department of Energy, one large coal-fired power plant generates 3 billion tons of $CO_2$ over the course of its lifetime and can dump almost 6 million tons (5.4 million metric tons) of $CO_2$ into the atmosphere in just one year. Since reducing $CO_2$ emissions is the main tactic for curbing climate change, it is significant that burning coal produces so much of it. "Kilowatt for kilowatt," says writer Jacob Leibenluft, "coal remains just about the most carbon-intensive energy source out there."[27] Indeed, the 600-some coal-fired power plants currently active in America produce 36 percent of the United States' total greenhouse gas emissions, according to the Environmental Protection Agency.

> " While coal was once viewed as a very dirty energy source, coal advocates say this fossil fuel has gotten increasingly cleaner and more efficient. "

## The Promise of Clean Coal

There might be a cleaner, brighter future for coal, however, one that is causing investors and politicians to give this fuel a new name: clean coal. "Clean coal" refers to a power plant technology called carbon capture and storage (CCS). Instead of releasing $CO_2$ from coal burning into the air, CCS power plants would separate up to 90 percent of the $CO_2$ and capture and store it so it is not released into the atmosphere. The $CO_2$ would then be liquefied and stored in large underground containers or sold to other industries that have a need for it (such as oil excavators, who can inject $CO_2$ into wells to push hard-to-reach oil up to the top).

Thus far such technology is only experimental, but coal executives are confident that such a technology can and will be developed soon. They are pushing the United States to build more coal-fired power plants. Says coal advocate Joe Lucas, "There has never been a technological challenge facing the coal-based sector where technology hasn't solved the problem."[28]

Given coal's low cost and abundant domestic supply, people want to invest in clean coal technology. According to a survey taken by the American Coalition for Clean Coal Electricity, 69 percent of Americans surveyed said that coal is an important fuel for America's future, and 84 percent said that developing clean coal technology offers valuable energy and job opportunities. As Senator John McCain put it during the 2008 presidential election campaign, "Perhaps no advancement in energy technology could mean more to America than the clean burning of coal and the capture and storage of carbon emissions."[29]

## Can Coal Ever Be Truly Clean?

Coal companies have spent millions on advertising clean coal, but the main problem is that, right now, there is no such thing: CCS technology does not yet exist and is not likely to come about for another 10 to 20 years. As a result, critics attack the messages sent by power companies like Dominion, which in 2008 ran ads promoting a facility that would, by 2012, be producing electricity with state-of-the-art clean coal technology. "What the unbuilt facility actually possesses," writes journalist Ben Elgin, "is a plot of land set aside for $CO_2$-removal technology—once it is invented and becomes commercially feasible."[30] Elgin and others believe that the technology might never become viable, and thus it is wrong to build more polluting power plants in anticipation of a technology that might never come to fruition.

> **Coal companies have spent millions on advertising clean coal, but the main problem is that right now, there is no such thing: CCS technology does not yet exist.**

Indeed, early reports indicate that carbon capture and storage may be incredibly difficult to achieve. Early efforts to develop CCS technology have not met with success: A government-sponsored plant called FutureGen, which was supposed to demonstrate the technology, has been so expensive that its funding is faltering and it is behind its original schedule.

One problem is that it would take an enormous amount of space to contain all of that captured $CO_2$. For example, to store the liquefied

$CO_2$ produced by one large coal-fired power plant, one would need a facility the size of a major oil field. Storing this material could prove to be impractical, too, as underground storage would be prone to earthquakes and leakage. Says former Energy Department adviser Curt M. White, "Red flags should be going up everywhere when you talk about this amount of liquid being put underground."[31]

Furthermore, such technology is incredibly expensive. The International Energy Agency has estimated that $20 billion is needed to research CCS technology properly. The cost of converting already existing power plants to CCS technology is estimated to be even higher: "By a conservative estimate, [it would cost] several trillion dollars to switch to clean coal in the U.S. alone,"[32] reports Elgin.

Finally, some say that coal can *never* be a truly clean energy source, even if its $CO_2$ outputs could be accounted for with CCS technology. This is because before coal is even burned, it has to be mined—and this is a dirty and dangerous process that levels mountains, pollutes land and water, and threatens the health and lives of miners. According to journalist Jeff Biggers, 1 million acres (404,686ha) of hardwood forests, 1,000 miles (1,609km) of waterways, and more than 460 mountains—an area that together equals that of the state of Delaware—have been depleted or destroyed by coal mining in the United States. "No matter how 'cap 'n trade' schemes pan out in the distant future for coal-fired plants, strip mining and underground coal mining remain the dirtiest and most destructive ways of making energy," says Biggers. "How much more death and destruction will it take to strip coal of this bright, shining, 'clean' lie?"[33]

Whether coal can ever truly be made clean and whether the burning of fossil fuels is contributing to climate change are just two of the environmental questions people raise over the use of fossil fuels. These discussions are likely to take center stage in the shaping of laws and policies about fossil fuel use in the coming years and decades.

# Primary Source Quotes*

## Does Fossil Fuel Use Threaten the Environment?

> **66** Scientists are certain that human activities are changing the composition of the atmosphere, and that increasing the concentration of greenhouse gases will change the planet's climate. **99**

—Environmental Protection Agency, "Climate Change," October 29, 2008. www.epa.gov.

The Environmental Protection Agency is a federal agency charged with safeguarding human health and the environment.

> **66** We don't know how or why climate changes. We do know it's changed dramatically throughout the planet's history, including the so-called 'little Ice Age' beginning in 600 . . . and that, by comparison, the industrial age has been a time of relative climate stability. **99**

—Mark Steyn, "Climate Change Myth," *Australian*, September 11, 2006. www.freerepublic.com.

Steyn is a Canadian columnist and political commentator.

Bracketed quotes indicate conflicting positions.

* Editor's Note: While the definition of a primary source can be narrowly or broadly defined, for the purposes of Compact Research, a primary source consists of: 1) results of original research presented by an organization or researcher; 2) eyewitness accounts of events, personal experience, or work experience; 3) first-person editorials offering pundits' opinions; 4) government officials presenting political plans and/or policies; 5) representatives of organizations presenting testimony or policy.

66 People are causing global warming by burning fossil fuels (like oil, coal and natural gas) and cutting down forests. Scientists have shown that these activities are pumping far more $CO_2$ into the atmosphere than was ever released in hundreds of thousands of years. This buildup of $CO_2$ is the biggest cause of global warming. 99

—Environmental Defense Fund, "Global Warming Myths and Facts," 2008. www.edf.org.

The Environmental Defense Fund is an environmental advocacy group known for its work on global warming, among other environmental issues.

66 Analysis of the best data of the past 30 years has convinced me that the human contribution [to climate change] has been insignificant—in spite of the real rise in atmospheric $CO_2$, a greenhouse gas. 99

—S. Fred Singer, in Deroy Murdock, "Chill Out on Climate Hysteria: The Earth Is Currently Cooling," *National Review*, May 2, 2008. www.nationalreview.com.

Singer is a professor of environmental sciences at the University of Virginia and the founding director of the U.S. Weather Satellite Service. Murdock is a columnist with the Scripps Howard News Service and a media fellow with the Hoover Institution.

66 We can come up with ways to clean up after coal . . . but coal itself is not clean and never will be. That is a matter of chemistry and geology. 99

—Steven Mufson, "The 'Clean Coal' Myth," *Newsweek/Washington Post*, October 2, 2008. http://newsweek.washingtonpost.com.

Mufson is the author of the online column Energy Wire, jointly published by *Newsweek* and the *Washington Post*.

**66** Investing in new coal-based power plants and advanced technologies that will be retrofitted to existing power plants will create thousands upon thousands of jobs for American workers. **99**

—Cullen West, "Michigan Should Follow Obama's Lead, and Get Behind Clean Coal Projects," *Bay City (MI) Times*, January 4, 2009. www.mlive.com.

West is communications director for the American Coalition for Clean Coal Electricity.

**66** There is *very high confidence* that the net effect of human activities since 1750 has been one of warming. . . . In order to stabilise the concentration of GHGs [greenhouse gases] in the atmosphere, emissions would need to peak and decline thereafter. **99**

—Intergovernmental Panel on Climate Change, "Climate Change 2007: Summary for Policymakers," 2007. www.ipcc.ch.

The Intergovernmental Panel on Climate Change is an international scientific committee charged by the United Nations with evaluating matters related to climate change.

**66** It is not established that it is possible to significantly alter global climate through cuts in human greenhouse gas emissions. On top of which, because attempts to cut emissions will slow development, the current UN approach of $CO_2$ reduction is likely to increase human suffering from future climate change rather than to decrease it. **99**

—"Open Letter to the Secretary-General of the United Nations," December 13, 2007. www.heartland.org.

Text from a letter to the UN secretary-general signed by 100 scientists voicing strong opposition to the United Nations' efforts to link fossil fuel use with climate change and cut $CO_2$ emissions accordingly.

❝For now—and for years to come—'clean coal' will remain more a catchphrase than a reality. Despite the eagerness of the coal and power industries to sanitize their image and the desire of U.S. politicians to push a healthy-sounding alternative to expensive foreign oil and natural gas, clean coal is still a misnomer.❞

—Ben Elgin, "The Dirty Truth About Clean Coal," *BusinessWeek*, June 19, 2008. www.businessweek.com.

Elgin is a correspondent for *BusinessWeek* magazine.

❝'Clean coal' is not some cheap buzzword used to pander to certain constituencies. Rather, it is an evolving concept that goes back more than three decades.❞

—Brad Jones, "Bright Future Depends on Electricity Prices," *Denver Post*, December 4, 2008. www.denverpost.com.

Jones is the western region communications director of the American Coalition for Clean Coal Electricity.

❝Clean coal: never was there an oxymoron more insidious, or more dangerous to our public health.❞

—Jeff Biggers, "'Clean' Coal? Don't Try to Shovel That," *Washington Post*, March 2, 2008. www.washingtonpost.com.

Biggers is the author of *The United States of Appalachia: How Southern Mountaineers Brought Independence, Culture and Enlightenment to America.*

❝Modern, state-of-the-art, low-pollution coal-fired generators have replaced both antiquated power plants and monstrous industrial furnaces. . . .They improve and save millions of lives.❞

—Paul Driessen, "Saving Lives with Coal," *Townhall*, January 3, 2008. http://townhall.com.

Driessen is the author of *Eco-Imperialism: Green Power—Black Death.*

# Does Fossil Fuel Use Threaten the Environment?

- According to the Intergovernmental Panel on Climate Change (IPCC):

  - During the twentieth century the global average surface temperature increased by about **1°F** (0.6°C)

  - Global sea levels increased about **6 to 8 inches** (15 to 20 cm)

  - The Earth's **climate will change faster** in the 100 years between 2000 and 2100 than in the last 10,000 years

- NASA's Goddard Institute for Space Studies says that average global temperatures have climbed **1.4°F** (0.8°C) around the world since 1880, much of this in recent decades.

- As recorded by all four agencies that track the Earth's temperature—the Hadley Climate Research Unit in Britain, the NASA Goddard Institute for Space Studies in New York, the Christy group at the University of Alabama, and Remote Sensing Systems Inc. in California:

  - The global average temperature **cooled** by about **1.25°F** (0.7°C) in 2007.

  - This is the **fastest temperature change** ever recorded and matched the global average temperature of 1930.

## Developing Nations Will Produce More $CO_2$ in the Future

The International Energy Agency predicts that 97 percent of the increase in $CO_2$ emissions between now and 2030 will come from developing nations such as China, India, and countries in the Middle East.

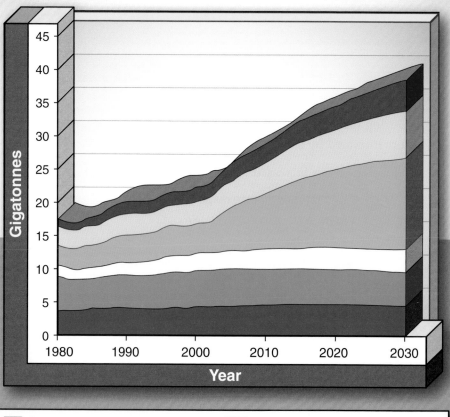

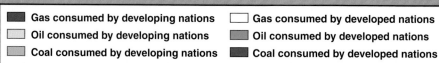

**Gas consumed by developing nations**    Gas consumed by developed nations
Oil consumed by developing nations    **Oil consumed by developed nations**
Coal consumed by developing nations    **Coal consumed by developed nations**

Source: World Energy Outlook, "Energy-Related $CO_2$ Emissions in the Reference Scenario," 2008.

# Cleaner Coal

$CO_2$ emissions from coal-fired power plants have been reduced by 77 percent over the last 35 years. Coal advocates believe that new technology called Carbon Capture and Storage (CCS) will further help reinvent coal as a clean, environmentally friendly energy source.

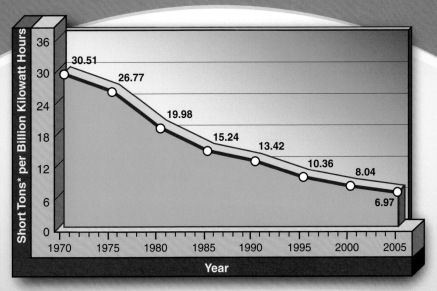

*A short ton is a unit of weight equal to about 2,000 pounds.

Source: U.S. Environmental Protection Agency "Overall Emissions/1970–2005," 2006.

- According to the National Oceanic and Atmospheric Administration, global levels of atmospheric carbon dioxide increased by **19 billion tons** (17 billion metric tons) in 2007, leaving a worldwide concentration of 385 parts per million. The level that is expected to herald disastrous climate change is 450 parts per million.

- A 2008 Harris poll found that **67 percent** of Americans believe that human activity is causing the global temperature to rise, while only **17 percent** of Americans believe that human activity has nothing to do with the problem.

# Human Activity Is Increasing Greenhouse Gases in the Environment

Increasing amounts of greenhouse gases—including carbon dioxide ($CO_2$), methane ($CH_4$), and nitrous oxide ($N_2O$)—are released into the atmosphere each year. The majority of these come from the burning of fossil fuels.

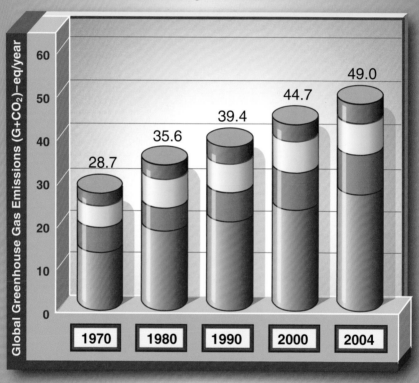

Global Greenhouse Gas Emissions (G+$CO_2$)–eq/year

| Year | Value |
|------|-------|
| 1970 | 28.7 |
| 1980 | 35.6 |
| 1990 | 39.4 |
| 2000 | 44.7 |
| 2004 | 49.0 |

$CO_2$ from fossil fuel use and other sources

$CO_2$ from deforestation, decay, and peat

$CH_4$ (methane) from fossil fuel use and other sources

$N_2O$ (nitrous oxide) from fossil fuel use and other sources

Source: Intergovernmental Panel on Climate Change, "Climate Change 2007: Summary for Policymakers," 2007. www.ipcc.ch.

- According to the Sierra Club, air pollution from the burning of coal accounts for at least **24,000 premature deaths** a year in the United States.

# The Climate Is Changing

Recent decades have seen an increase in the Earth's average surface temperature, a rise in its average sea level, and a decrease in snow cover in the Northern Hemisphere. Experts are not in agreement, however, on whether these changes are natural or the result of human activity.

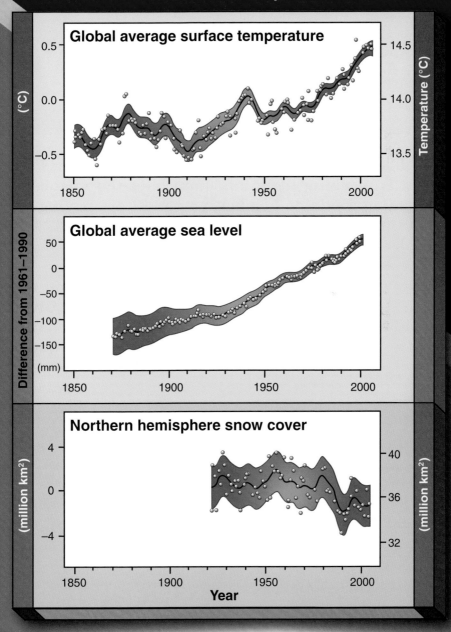

Source: Intergovernmental Panel on Climate Change, "Climate Change 2007: Summary for Policymakers," 2007. www.ipcc.ch.

51

# How Does Fossil Fuel Use Affect National Security?

66When a Wahhabi *madrassa* [religious school] in Pakistan is teaching little Pakistani boys the virtues of becoming a suicide bomber, you and I are paying for that through our gasoline prices.99

—R. James Woolsey, former director of the Central Intelligence Agency.

66Belief that cutting oil profits would cut Islamic terrorism is a matter of faith, not a matter of fact. Given the low-cost nature of terrorism, there is little chance that anyone's energy policy is going to bother al Qaeda very much.99

—Jerry Taylor and Peter Van Doren, senior fellows at the Cato Institute.

The United States imports about 64 percent of its oil from foreign sources. America's heavy foreign fossil fuel consumption has been blamed for keeping it engaged in protracted, bloody, expensive "resource wars" and for making it and its allies the targets of terrorism. For this reason, America's dependence on fossil fuels has been billed as not only an environmental and economic issue, but a national security one as well.

According to Resources for the Future, an environmental think tank,

3 of every 5 barrels of oil sold on the global market come from insecure areas such as the Persian Gulf, North Africa, Nigeria, Angola, Venezuela, Russia, and the Caspian states, most of which are outwardly hostile to the United States. The Middle East, for example—where the United States gets 20 percent of the oil it imports—is a notoriously war-torn region filled with dictatorships, religious extremists, and terrorists. The instability and violence of the region complicates America's need to buy a product from them. As Professor John Scire has put it, "[Oil] wouldn't be a national security issue if all the oil came from safe places like Canada and Mexico, but it doesn't."[34] When oil is located in the same regions that are perpetually plagued by war, political instability, and terrorism, the United States becomes financially and militarily entangled to protect its access to this critical resource.

That the United States gets so much of its oil from unfriendly and unsafe places is said to affect its national security by making it vulnerable to terrorist attacks. Oil can be one of several reasons the United States gets involved in the affairs of other nations. This is in part what motivated Osama bin Laden to attack the United States—because he resents U.S. involvement in his home country of Saudi Arabia. In fact, U.S. addiction to oil has been cited by terrorists as a reason to attack Americans both at home and abroad. As al Qaeda deputy leader Ayman al-Zawahiri said in a taped message released in December 2005, "I call on the Mujahideen [Islamic holy warriors] to concentrate their attacks on . . . stolen oil, most of the revenues of which go to the enemies of Islam while most of

> **America's dependence on fossil fuels has been billed as not only an environmental and economic issue, but a national security one as well.**

what they leave is seized by the thieves who run our countries."[35] Bin Laden has made similar statements when he rationalizes terrorist attacks on U.S. soil and citizens. "The lethal threat from terrorism," says scholar Michael T. Klare, "therefore cannot be separated from our reliance on foreign oil."[36]

The oil industry itself is vulnerable to security breaches and attacks.

Oil facilities, installations, personnel, and pipelines are among the most common targets of terrorist attacks. This is especially true in Iraq. Since the start of the Iraq War in March 2003, these places have been attacked more than 469 times. Not only do these attacks disrupt the flow of oil and cost millions in lost business, they also cause heavy damage to infrastructure and kill hundreds of people.

## Held Hostage by Foreign Oil

Yet another way in which it is said that dependence on foreign oil hampers national security is that it prevents the United States from adequately responding to threats from abroad when those threats are tied up with the oil supply. For example, the United States has been involved in an ongoing conflict with Iran over that nation's increasingly hostile stance to the United States and its allies, and many suspect it is secretly making nuclear weapons in violation of international law. "Yet efforts to respond to this threat with multilateral sanctions have foundered on fears that Iran would retaliate by withholding oil from world markets," explains David B. Sandalow, energy scholar at the Brookings Institution. In this way, he says, "we remain hostage to our continuing dependence on oil."[37]

> " U.S. addiction to oil has been cited by terrorists as a reason to attack Americans both at home and abroad. "

Iran is not the only place in which America's foreign oil dependence requires it to operate with one hand tied behind its back. Saudi Arabia—where 15 of the 19 hijackers on September 11 were from—is also the second-largest supplier of oil to the United States. In 2008 the United States imported more than 1.4 million barrels per day from the Saudis. It is argued that the United States can't buy oil and fight terrorism in the same place at the same time—because it needs Saudi oil so much, it can't make a significant attempt to destabilize that country by fighting terrorism there.

## Funding Terrorism with Petrodollars

The enormous sum of money spent on oil is another way in which oil's use is said to threaten American national security. America's foreign oil purchases cost an estimated $150 billion to $200 billion each year. Payments for Saudi Arabia's oil alone amount to $51 billion a year, and the Saudis, among others, do not necessarily buy American products in return. "As a result, the American economy loses $150 billion every year and that money only increases other countries' competitiveness,"[38] says Scire. Since a strong economy typically goes hand in hand with a strong military, the bleeding of American dollars abroad hampers America's ability to protect itself.

Not only does the United States not reabsorb this money in purchases of its products and services, but some suspect that significant portions of this money actually make their way to terrorists, who in turn use it to commit attacks against America and its allies. The huge flow of oil money is believed to finance terrorist networks, paying for their schools, weapons, and other materials. Much of this money is filtered through charitable donations from people who have no loyalty to the United States but profit from its oil purchases. As

> " Another way in which it is said that dependence on foreign oil hampers national security is that it prevents the United States from adequately responding to threats from abroad when those threats are tied up with the oil supply. "

Klare explains, "Growing dependency [on foreign oil] compels us to coddle foreign oil potentates like the royal family of Saudi Arabia—some of whose members made lavish donations to Islamic charities linked to Osama bin Laden and al Qaeda."[39] That American petrodollars are being funneled to the people who would most harm Americans is among the most frequently and passionately made points about how foreign oil dependence compromises national security.

## United States Is Vulnerable to Disruption in Oil Distribution

A scenario run by a bipartisan panel of intelligence, military, and energy experts in 2005 demonstrates the extent to which the United States is made vulnerable by its dependence on foreign oil. The panel ran a cri-

> " That American petrodollars are being funneled to the people who would most harm Americans is among the most passionately made points about how foreign oil dependence compromises national security. "

sis exercise called Oil Shockwave that simulated an attack on an Alaskan oil facility, unrest in Nigeria, and an emergency in Saudi Arabia. The simulators predicted that such an event would drive the price of oil to over $150 per barrel and significantly interrupt global supply. Although the simulation only affected about 4 percent of the oil sold every day, it showed catastrophic results. Among these were 2 million lost jobs, gasoline prices of $5.74 per gallon (3.8L), and an emboldening of oil-producing countries that would result in China and Saudi Arabia being able to blackmail the United States into changing its foreign policy toward nations like Taiwan and Israel.

Simulations about the future show one way in which the United States might be blackmailed as a result of its foreign oil dependence, and history shows another. In 1973 the Arab oil-exporting nations refused to sell oil to the United States to punish it for supporting the state of Israel. The U.S. economy was thrown into turmoil—the price of oil quadrupled, the stock market plunged, and millions of Americans experienced gas shortages.

## Drilling in Alaska's Arctic Wildlife Refuge

To avoid funding terrorists, fighting resource wars, being blackmailed with oil, and experiencing the other problems that come with depending on foreign oil, it has been suggested that America open up domestic sources for exploration and drilling. In particular, Alaska's Arctic National Wildlife Refuge (ANWR) has been targeted for this purpose. Located in northeastern Alaska, ANWR is one of the last untouched wildernesses on Earth. It is also believed to contain large oil reserves that could be of great use to Americans.

Those in favor of opening the region to oil exploration claim that drilling will offer the United States much-needed energy independence and security. The region is expected to hold as much as 10.4 billion barrels of crude oil. According to a 2008 report published by the Energy Information Administration, if ANWR were opened immediately, oil could be flowing by 2018 and reach a peak of 780,000 barrels a day by 2027. As of early 2009 ANWR had still not been opened to drilling and exploration, frustrating those who want to see the United States take direct action to wean itself off foreign oil. Says commentator Joe Bell, "If Congress had opened ANWR to drilling a decade ago the nation would be that much closer to lessening its dependency on foreign oil today. America cannot afford to be saying that a decade from now."[40]

## Detractors of Arctic Drilling

But others are less convinced that drilling in ANWR would meaningfully reduce America's reliance on foreign oil. For one, even if ANWR were opened to oil production tomorrow, it is estimated to take about 10 years to explore, excavate, and drill for it. Once the oil was recovered, it would need to be refined and transported to the lower 48 states via the Trans-Alaska Pipeline (which itself is vulnerable to terrorist attack). At this rate, experts do not expect oil from ANWR to offer significant relief from foreign oil imports until the year 2030—at which point oil production in ANWR would also begin to decline.

Secondly, it is unclear how much oil could actually be recovered from ANWR or whether it would be enough to help America provide for its own energy needs. The 10.4 billion barrels of recoverable oil in the refuge does

> " It is unclear how much oil could actually be recovered from ANWR or whether it would be enough to help America provide for its own energy needs. "

not seem like very much when one considers that in 2008 Americans were consuming more than 20 million barrels of oil a day. Furthermore, officials at the Energy Information Administration claim the amount of oil recovered from ANWR would only amount to between 0.4 and 1.2 percent of total world oil consumption—not enough to make a significant difference.

Furthermore, the oil from ANWR—though produced domestically—would not lower the cost of oil significantly enough to offer Americans financial relief. Best-case scenarios from the Energy Information Administration in 2008 put the cost savings of ANWR oil at $1.44 per barrel, and these would not be realized until at least 2027. This is due in part to the fact that oil prices are determined by the world market (not just an American one), and in part to the fact that getting the oil out of ANWR is likely to be an enormously expensive endeavor in itself.

## The Oil-National Security Myth

Opening ANWR to drilling seems especially unhelpful if one rejects the theory that oil is a national security issue in the first place, as significant numbers of people do. Increasingly, analysts are casting doubt on the conventional wisdom that links oil and national security, claiming that America's foreign dependence on oil might be an economic issue, but not one of national security.

> **The fact that modern terrorist attacks are incredibly cheap to execute . . . is one reason to doubt the connection between petrodollars and terrorism.**

That unfriendly nations might use oil as a weapon or to blackmail the United States is disputed by Reason Foundation analyst Shikha Dalmia, who points out that while the Arab nations did attempt to do just that in 1973, they were not very successful. The embargo lasted just a few months, in part because the United States was able to get oil from other sources. The long lines at gas stations were more a product of national panic than actual oil shortages, suggests Dalmia.

Furthermore, it is debated whether oil money has anything to do with causing or funding terrorism. The fact that modern terrorist attacks are incredibly cheap to execute—some cost no more than a few thousand dollars—is one reason to doubt the connection between petrodollars and terrorism. Explain Cato Institute fellows Jerry Taylor and Peter Van Doren: "Terrorists don't need oil revenues. The fact that catastrophic terrorism can be undertaken on the proverbial dime (a few hundred thousand dollars paid for the 9/11 attacks) suggests that choking off financial resources to al Qaeda effectively is a hopeless task."[41]

Taylor, Van Doren, and others suggest that withdrawing oil money from the countries where terrorists are known to operate might actually make things worse for U.S. security. The less money spent in these countries, the more their citizens lose their income—and the more likely it is they will become resentful of the United States and subscribe to the radicalized anti-American sentiments of terrorists. "To the extent that deteriorating economic conditions breed social discontent and political resentment," say Taylor and Van Doren, "'starving the oil beast' might well increase the recruitment pool for al Qaeda and invite producer states to reconsider their allegiances in the war on terror."[42] Clearly, whether foreign oil helps or hurts U.S. security is one of the many debates surrounding its use.

# How Does Fossil Fuel Use Affect National Security?

66 **Wealthy Saudi financiers and charities have funded terrorist organizations and causes that support terrorism and the ideology that fuels the terrorists' agenda.** 99

—Stuart Levey, testimony before the Senate Committee on Banking, Housing, and Urban Affairs, July 13, 2005. www.treasury.gov.

Levey is the first undersecretary for terrorism and financial intelligence, a branch of the U.S. Department of the Treasury.

..................................................................................................................................

66 **Everything we know suggests that al Qaeda terrorist cells are 'pay as you go' operations that primarily engage in garden-variety crime to fund their activities. [The] governments of Saudi Arabia, Kuwait, and others in the region . . . have no interest in facilitating the transfer of oil revenues to some post office box in Pakistan.** 99

—Jerry Taylor and Peter Van Doren, "Driving Bin Laden? Oil Consumption Has Little to Do with Terrorism," *National Review*, March 8, 2006. www.nationalreview.com.

Taylor and Van Doren are fellows at the Cato Institute, a libertarian think tank concerned with matters of liberty, free market, and international relations.

..................................................................................................................................

Bracketed quotes indicate conflicting positions.

\* Editor's Note: While the definition of a primary source can be narrowly or broadly defined, for the purposes of Compact Research, a primary source consists of: 1) results of original research presented by an organization or researcher; 2) eyewitness accounts of events, personal experience, or work experience; 3) first-person editorials offering pundits' opinions; 4) government officials presenting political plans and/or policies; 5) representatives of organizations presenting testimony or policy.

66 **It's increasingly likely that oil-producing states may try to use oil as a weapon with which to achieve political goals. . . . It [is] much more likely that an oil producing state with a political axe to grind will cut output to certain customers.** 99

—Ian Bremmer, "Prices Transform Oil into a Weapon," *International Herald Tribune*, August 27, 2005. www.iht.com.

Bremmer is president of the Eurasia Group and a senior fellow at the World Policy Institute.

66 **The Iranian government depends on oil exports for nearly half of its total revenues. If it cuts these exports, buyers could go to other suppliers. But there is not much else that Iran could sell to other countries to replace its lost oil revenues.** 99

—Shikha Dalmia, "Defend America, Buy More Iranian Oil," Reason Foundation, May 5, 2006. www.reason.org.

Dalmia is a senior analyst at the Reason Foundation, an institute that promotes individual liberty and limited government.

66 **There could be as many as 11.8 billion barrels of oil beneath ANWR's coastal plain. . . . Given our growing dependence on foreign oil and the predicted spike in heating costs this winter, it would be plainly irresponsible for Congress to cower to green caterwauling and put America's energy security on hold.** 99

—Peyton Knight, "ANWR: To Drill or Not to Drill? There Is No Question." National Policy Analysis No. 535, National Center for Public Policy Research, December 2005. www.nationalcenter.org.

Knight is the director of environmental and regulatory affairs at the National Center for Public Policy Research.

66 **Over 50 times as much oil as might be under the Arctic Refuge, at very high prices, can be saved at very low prices by using the oil efficiently.** 99

—Amory Lovins, in Janice Mason, "Arctic National Wildlife Refuge (ANWR): Why Not Drill in ANWR for Oil? Creating a Renewable Future," *Estes Park (CO) Trail-Gazette*, July 25, 2008. www.eptrail.com.

Lovins is the cofounder, chair, and chief scientist of the Rocky Mountain Institute in Colorado.

**❝Because we depend so completely on oil, we devote extraordinary political and military resources to securing it, at staggering cost. We empower oil-exporting nations that wish us ill.❞**

—David B. Sandalow, "Ending Oil Dependence: Protecting National Security, the Environment, and the Economy," Brookings Institution, 2008. www.brookings.edu.

Sandalow is an energy and environment scholar and a senior fellow at the Brookings Institution.

**❝The oft-stated objective of 'energy independence' is as devoid of substance and irrelevant to our security as 'computer independence' or 'clothing independence.' . . . Politicians and pundits alike would do well to put this treasured, but frayed, idea aside.❞**

—Phillip E. Auerswald, "Calling an End to Oil Alarmism," *Boston Globe*, January 23, 2007. http://belfercenter.ksg.harvard.edu.

Auerswald is the director of the Center for Science and Technology Policy at George Mason University's School of Public Policy and a research associate at the Belfer Center for Science and International Affairs at the Kennedy School of Government at Harvard University.

# Facts and Illustrations

## How Does Fossil Fuel Use Affect National Security?

- According to the Heritage Foundation:
  - The United States is the largest oil importer in the world, bringing in **13.5 million barrels** each day from foreign sources.
  - **64 percent** of total U.S. daily consumption comes from foreign sources.
  - **20 percent** of U.S. foreign oil imports come from the Middle East.

- According to the Energy Information Administration:
  - In 1974 the United States imported just **35 percent** of its oil.
  - By 2017 the United States will be importing **68 percent** of its oil needs.
  - By 2027 it will be importing **70 percent** of its oil needs.

- According to the U.S. Department of Energy, the United States imports oil from the following unstable or unfriendly nations:
  - **1.4 million** barrels per day from Saudi Arabia
  - **800,000** barrels per day from other Persian Gulf states
  - **1.4 million** barrels per day from Venezuela
  - **1.1 million** barrels per day from Nigeria

- According to the environmental group US PIRG, drilling in ANWR would reduce gasoline prices by **less than a penny and a half a gallon** (3.8L), and not until 2025.

# Buying Our Oil from Abroad

The United States imports more than 60 percent of its oil from foreign sources—but not all of these nations are friendly to the United States, or run by stable governments.

**1). Canada**
Exports 2,028 barrels to U.S.

**8). Algeria**
Exports 381 barrels to U.S. Relations with the U.S. are currently friendly, but Algeria has a long history of civil war and military leadership

**6). Iraq**
Exports 452 barrels to U.S. Invaded by the U.S. in 2003

**10). Kuwait**
Exports 272 barrels to U.S. The invasion of Kuwait by Iraq in 1991 was the cause of the first Gulf War, led by the U.S.

**3). Mexico**
Exports 1,296 barrels to U.S.

**4). Venezuela**
Exports 1,071 barrels to U.S. Experienced increase in tensions with U.S. in 2006

**9). Brazil**
Exports 280 barrels to U.S.

**5). Nigeria**
Exports 775 barrels to U.S. Plagued by ethnic violence in the Niger Delta region, the area where oil is produced

**7). Angola**
Exports 438 barrels to U.S. Devastated by decades of civil war

**2). Saudi Arabia**
Exports 1,461 barrels to U.S. Home of 15 of the 9/11 hijackers, and birthplace of Osama bin Laden

Note: Number in thousands of barrels per day

Source: Energy Information Administration, "Crude Oil and Total Petroleum Imports Top 15 Countries," January 15, 2009. www.eia.doe.gov.

- The first time an environmental matter was officially linked with national security was when the **National Security Strategy**—the document that periodically updates the nation's official position on national security—was issued in the early 1990s by President George H.W. Bush.

# Increasing Demand for Energy Creates Conflict

The worldwide demand for energy is expected to increase by 45 percent between now and 2030. As more nations fight over the remaining supply of fossil fuels, "resource wars" are expected to become more common, as are energy shortages that could spread chaos and instability.

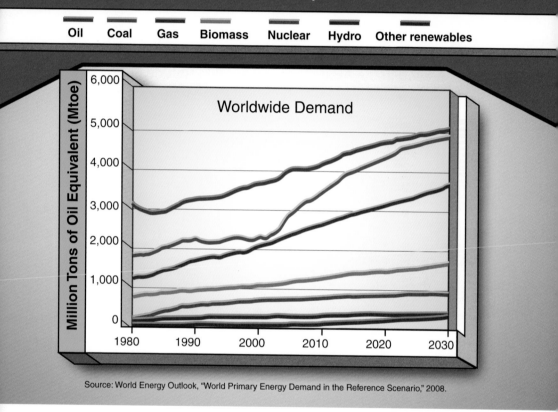

Oil    Coal    Gas    Biomass    Nuclear    Hydro    Other renewables

Source: World Energy Outlook, "World Primary Energy Demand in the Reference Scenario," 2008.

- Since the administration of President Bill Clinton (1993–2001), there has been an **environmental officer** in the National Security Council.

# American Opinions on Drilling in ANWR

Americans go back and forth on whether they support opening Alaska's Arctic National Wildlife Refuge for oil exploration and drilling. Supporters claim such a move could help lessen America's dependence on foreign oil, which might keep it safe from terrorism and the whims of other countries. Others argue its impact will be insignificant and not worth the effort.

**"Would you favor or oppose allowing oil and gas drilling in the Arctic National Wildlife Refuge in Alaska?"**

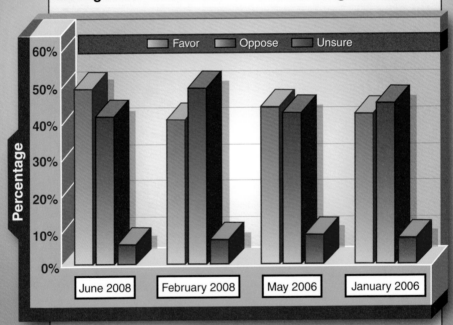

Source: Pew Research Center for the People & the Press survey conducted by Princeton Survey Research Associates International. June 18–29, 2008.

# Can Alternative Energy Sources Replace Fossil Fuels?

No energy source offers the convenience, availability, and power of fossil fuels, which is why the world continues to rely so heavily on them. However, given the environmental, security, and supply issues associated with their use, the twenty-first century has witnessed a push to explore alternative sources of energy. Renewable resources such as wind, solar, and biofuels, as well as nuclear power, are all touted as replacements for fossil fuels. Each of these energy sources has benefits— but also drawbacks. Taken together these benefits and drawbacks will determine to what extent alternative energy sources might take the place of fossil fuels.

# Nuclear Power Generates Tremendous Power

Nuclear power is increasingly discussed as an alternative to fossil fuels because it is a fantastically effective energy source. Very few other energy sources are able to generate such a tremendous amount of power. According to authors Peter W. Huber and Mark P. Mills, the amount of nuclear fuel rods needed to power the entire city of Manhattan could fit in a single two-bedroom apartment. "Furnaces, espresso machines, subways, streetlights, stock tickers, Times Square, everything," say Huber and Mills. "Two rooms' worth of fuel could electrify it all."[43] Nuclear energy's powerful punch is one reason it provides 8.5 percent of the United States' total energy needs, and 20 percent of its electricity, and why supporters would like it to supply even more.

> "Nuclear power is increasingly discussed as an alternative to fossil fuels because it is a fantastically effective energy source."

While in past decades the radiation emitted by nuclear power plants was a significant obstacle to its use, it is now estimated that less than 1 percent of the public's exposure to radiation comes from nuclear power plants, rendering them a safe source of power. According to the Heritage Foundation, about 83 percent of the radiation a person is exposed to annually comes from natural sources such as cosmic rays, uranium in the Earth's crust, and radioactive gas in the atmosphere. The rest comes from medical procedures such as X-rays, and about 3 percent from consumer products. "The Department of Energy reports that living near a nuclear power plant exposes a person to 1 millirem of radiation a year. By comparison, an airline passenger who flies from New York to Los Angeles receives 2.5 millirem," explain analysts Jack Spencer and Nicolas Loris. "Radiation exposure from living near a nuclear power plant is insignificant."[44]

Another selling point of nuclear power is the fact that it does not produce the kinds of greenhouse gases emitted by burning fossil fuels. In recent years nuclear power has been billed as a "green" energy source because it does not release $CO_2$ into the air when produced. For those who see the reduction of greenhouse gas emissions as the key to reducing global warming, nuclear power is therefore an increasingly attractive option. Even the cofounder of Greenpeace, Patrick Moore, is now one of nuclear power's most enthusiastic proponents. "I once opposed nuclear energy. But times have changed, and new facts of compelling importance have emerged," says Moore. "Nuclear energy holds the greatest potential to arrest the dangers we face from global warming. It is the only non-greenhouse-gas-emitting power source capable of effectively replacing fossil fuels and satisfying growing demand."[45]

## How "Green" Is Nuclear Power?

But to say nuclear energy is a "green" source of power is not entirely accurate either. For one thing, nuclear power generates toxic waste that remains dangerous for thousands of years. Although waste can be stored in holding tanks, these could leak into the surrounding environment, causing cancer and birth defects. Secondly, nuclear power relies on uranium and plutonium, both highly radioactive elements that need to be mined and processed. And while the production of nuclear power does not directly cause any $CO_2$ emissions, the mining of these elements does, because their mining and processing requires the burning of fossil fuels.

In fact, when the environmental impact of mining is added to the picture, a 1,250 megawatt nuclear power plant produces the equivalent of 250,000 tons (226,796 metric tons) of carbon dioxide a year during its life, according to German researcher Uwe Fritsche, who has conducted thorough life-cycle analyses of nuclear power plants. Says author Helen Caldicott, "If you take the whole fuel chain as one piece, nuclear power produces large quantities of global warming gases because millions of tons of rock and ore need to be mined to get the uranium out of the ground. And it has to be crushed, using more fossil fuels."[46] Finally, uranium is itself a finite resource, one which the International Atomic Energy Agency predicts will run out in about 80 years. From this perspective, nuclear power is not much of an alternative to fossil fuels.

> " To say nuclear energy is a 'green' source of power is not entirely accurate. "

Furthermore, it is argued that nuclear power is vulnerable to dangerous accidents and even to terrorism. Nuclear power plants require the storage and processing of volatile materials to produce energy, and as such are a natural target for terrorists. It is feared that terrorists might infiltrate a plant and steal radioactive material with which to make a bomb. Even if the bomb were small, it could still kill and sicken thousands if it were exploded in a densely populated area. Or terrorists could turn a nuclear plant into a bomb itself by flying a plane into it. Tons of radioactive gases would be released in such an explosion, killing and sickening thousands of people in the surrounding area. Journalist Sherwood Ross paints the following picture of such an event:

> About 17 million people live within a 50 mile radius of the two Indian Point reactors in Buchanan, N.Y., just 35 miles from Manhattan. Suicidal terrorists . . . could disrupt the plant's electricity supply by ramming a speedboat packed with explosives into their Hudson River intake pipes. . . . Over time, the subsequent meltdown could claim an estimated 518,000 lives.[47]

Finally, it is feared that terrorists could take over a nuclear power plant from the inside. Mock terror drills conducted by the Nuclear Regulatory Commission (NRC) have revealed serious breaches in security, even since September 11. NRC agents posing as terrorists were able to enter several nuclear power plants without the knowledge of plant officials. Given this, author Regina S. Axelrod is among those calling for tighter security in and around nuclear power plants. "Since September 11th, safety and terrorism at nuclear power plants continue to be major concerns,"[48] says Axelrod.

> "Renewable sources of energy are infinite, meaning they come from sources that are continually replenished."

Yet many others argue it is unrealistic to worry that terrorists might use nuclear power plants as part of an attack. Most power plants are extremely well-guarded, and even if terrorists were able to penetrate them, it is unlikely they would be able to steal enough enriched uranium or plutonium for a bomb. Fears of an attack on a power plant by air or water are also often dismissed as being unreasonable, as since September 11, airport security has improved to the point where planes are unlikely to be hijacked and flown into direct targets. Even if a hijacking were to occur, Heritage Foundation analysts Jack Spencer and Nicolas Loris say it is unlikely a catastrophic explosion would result. "Nuclear reactors are designed to withstand the impact of airborne objects like passenger airplanes," they say, "and the Nuclear Regulatory Commission has increased security at U.S. nuclear power plants and has instituted other safeguards."[49] Spencer and Loris point out that the United States has 104 commercial nuclear power plants, and there are 446 worldwide—and not one of them has ever been involved in a successful terrorist attack. As a result, Spencer, Loris, and many others argue that fear of terrorism should not prevent the development of a potentially clean and efficient non–fossil fuel energy source.

> **Wyoming's wind potential alone is equal to the energy produced by all 104 U.S. nuclear power plants combined.**

## Renewable Resources to the Rescue?

Renewable resources are not prone to terrorist attack, and thus are seen as a safer alternative energy source than both nuclear power and fossil fuels. But the biggest benefit of renewable energy sources is that there are relatively no greenhouse gases or toxic substances associated with their use. Unlike fossil fuels, which emit climate-changing gases into the atmosphere, and nuclear power, which produces toxic waste, renewables like wind and solar power produce no environmentally dangerous by-products.

Also, unlike coal, natural gas, oil, and nuclear power, renewable sources of energy are infinite, meaning they come from sources that are continually replenished. Their renewable nature and their lack of pollution make renewables a very attractive power source to some. As reporter Joseph Romm puts it, "After capital costs, wind power and solar power are pretty much free—nobody charges for the breeze and the sun."[50]

That renewable power can be generated in America is another of its selling points. Unlike fossil fuels, which are largely imported, wind,

> It is likely that America's future energy program will be an amalgam of many energy sources.

solar, hydropower, and biofuels can all be made at home, offering the United States independence from foreign oil. Wind turbines can be erected in America's vast plains or off its many miles of coastlines. Solar panels, too, can harness the sun's power in the vast expanses of the American desert, or even on the rooftops of buildings in especially sunshine-filled states. Corn, soy, palm, and other plant matter that goes into the production of biofuels can be grown in the spacious fields and farms that make up America's corn belt. Each of these energy sources can help the United States develop a domestic energy program while at the same time curbing pollution.

## Concerns About Renewable Resources Potential

But there is much controversy over whether renewable sources of energy can provide the staggering amounts of fuel needed to power the United States. Some areas are naturally better suited to benefit from renewable sources of energy than others. For example, wind, solar, and water (for generating hydropower) are plentiful in the Midwest and can provide residents of that area with reliable and adequate energy. According to Arjun Makhijani, president of the Institute for Energy and Environmental Research, Wyoming's wind potential alone is equal to the energy produced by all 104 U.S. nuclear power plants combined.

But while they may have a lot of potential, renewable sources of energy have yet to, in reality, make a significant contribution to America's energy needs. According to the Energy Information Administration, as of 2008 all renewable sources of energy—wind, solar, biofuels, geothermal, hydroelectric, and wood-derived fuel—together provided just 7 percent of the nation's total energy. Individually, solar and wind power each provide less than 1 percent of the nation's total energy needs each year.

One reason renewables are used less often than nuclear power or fossil fuel is cost. While the price of renewable power has fallen in recent years, as of 2008 solar power still cost about 15 to 17 cents per kilowatt hour, compared with electricity generated from coal, which cost only 3 to 4 cents per kilowatt hour. Opponents of renewable sources of power also argue that millions of acres of land would need to be paved to make room for the thousands of solar panels and wind turbines that would have to be erected to effectively capture enough wind or sun to power just a few medium-size cities. According to one study, it would take 9 million acres (3.6 million ha) of land to power the entire country—this would require paving an area larger than the size of Connecticut, New Jersey, and Delaware combined.

In constructing these mammoth energy-harnessing devices, the habitat of thousands of species would be destroyed. In California's Mojave Desert, for example, vast solar panel fields are being erected that require enormous amounts of water and cement, which threaten habitat and interfere with the way the desert absorbs $CO_2$ from the atmosphere (which helps avoid global warming). It is for this reason that Amy Leinbach Marquis, writing for the National Parks Conservation Association, has said, "California's solar boom threatens the very places it's meant to protect."[51]

## A Multifaceted Energy Program

While renewable energy sources and nuclear power offer some advantages over fossil fuels, it is likely that America's future energy program will be an amalgam of many energy sources. Because of their efficiency, power, cost, and in-place infrastructure, fossil fuels are unlikely to be abandoned as an energy source. But they will probably be used in conjunction with renewable sources and nuclear power, even as they themselves are conserved. For example, cars of the future might run partially on gas and partially on electricity generated from a nearby nuclear power grid, or run part of the time on a hydrogen fuel cell, or be powered by biofuels. This is just one of the ways in which making fossil fuels work more efficiently and in conjunction with other fuel sources can help America meet its future energy needs.

# Can Alternative Energy Sources Replace Fossil Fuels?

> **" Nuclear power's main emission, of course, is massive quantities of radioactive waste that pollute food chains and cause cancer for hundreds of millions of years. "**

—Helen Caldicott, in Elsa Wenzel, "Nuke Power Not So Green or Clean," CNET News, June 11, 2007. http://news.cnet.com.

Caldicott is the author of the book *Nuclear Power Is Not the Answer*. Wenzel is a staff writer for CNET News.

...................................................................................................................................

> **" Spent nuclear fuel can be removed from the reactor, reprocessed to separate unused fuel, and then used again. . . . The argument that there is no solution to the waste problem is simply wrong. "**

—Jack Spencer and Nicolas Loris, "Dispelling Myths About Nuclear Energy," *Backgrounder*, Heritage Foundation, December 3, 2007. www.heritage.org.

Spencer and Loris work at the Thomas A. Roe Institute for Economic Policy Studies at the Heritage Foundation, a think tank devoted to the principles of free enterprise, limited government, individual freedom, and traditional American values.

...................................................................................................................................

Bracketed quotes indicate conflicting positions.

* Editor's Note: While the definition of a primary source can be narrowly or broadly defined, for the purposes of Compact Research, a primary source consists of: 1) results of original research presented by an organization or researcher; 2) eyewitness accounts of events, personal experience, or work experience; 3) first-person editorials offering pundits' opinions; 4) government officials presenting political plans and/or policies; 5) representatives of organizations presenting testimony or policy.

"Nuclear energy generates more than 70 percent of all carbon-free electricity in America and is an essential part of a technology-based solution for reducing greenhouse gases."

—Nuclear Energy Institute, "Nuclear Energy Plays Essential Role in Reducing Greenhouse Gas Emissions," July 2008. www.nei.org.

The Nuclear Energy Institute is the policy organization of the nuclear energy and technologies industry.

"Nuclear power's very limited ability to reduce greenhouse gases, compared to reductions that can be achieved using the same dollars for sustainable energy, and its enormously dangerous proliferation and pollution issues, combine to make nuclear an untenable, irrational energy choice."

—Alice Slater, "Nuclear Power No Solution to Global Warming," *Pacifist Ecologist*, Winter 2008. www.wagingpeace.org.

Slater is the New York director of the Nuclear Age Peace Foundation.

"You could supply the entire U.S. with the sun power here in a little piece of the Southwest."

—Dan Kabel, in Mark Clayton, "New Rays of Hope for Solar Power's Future," *Christian Science Monitor*, August 22, 2008. http://features.csmonitor.com.

Kabel is chief executive of Acciona Solar Power. Clayton is a staff writer for the *Christian Science Monitor*.

"New solar power capacity is triple the cost of new gas-generated electricity and quadruple the cost of surplus power. Solar power, like most other renewables, is geographically limited for the foreseeable future."

—Robert L. Bradley Jr., "Why Renewable Energy Is Not Cheap and Not Green," National Center for Policy Analysis, 2008. www.ncpa.org.

Bradley is president of the Institute for Energy Research in Houston and the author of *Oil, Gas, and Government: The U.S. Experience*.

66 Wind parks in [offshore] waters can generate more energy than nearshore and onshore sites, they don't ruin seascape views, and they don't interfere as much with other ocean activities. 99

—Emily Waltz, "Offshore Wind May Power the Future," *Scientific American*, October 20, 2008. www.sciam.com.

Waltz is a science journalist whose work has been published in *Nature Biotechnology*, *Plenty*, and *Scientific American*.

66 The opening up of the North Sea continental shelf to 7,000 wind turbines is, essentially, the building of a huge industrial infrastructure across a vast swathe of ecologically sensitive seabed—as 'unsustainable' in its own way as the opening of the Arctic Wildlife Refuge to oil exploration. 99

—Rob Johnston, "Ten Myths About Nuclear Power," *Spiked*, January 9, 2008. www.spiked-online.com.

Johnston is a writer who frequently comments on health, science, and environmental issues.

66 The energy challenges our country faces are severe and have gone unaddressed for far too long. Our addiction to foreign oil doesn't just undermine our national security and wreak havoc on our environment—it cripples our economy and strains the budgets of working families all across America. 99

—The White House, "The Agenda: Energy and the Environment," January 2009. www.whitehouse.gov.

The White House Web site presents the Obama administration's positions on energy and many other issues.

# Facts and Illustrations

## Can Alternative Energy Sources Replace Fossil Fuels?

- According to the Energy Information Administration:

  - The largest share of renewable-generated electricity comes from:

    - hydroelectric energy (**71 percent**)

    - biomass (**16 percent**)

    - wind (**9 percent**)

    - geothermal (**4 percent**)

    - solar (**0.2 percent**)

  - Most renewable energy is used to produce electricity. Electricity producers consumed more than half—**51 percent**—of the total renewable energy in 2007.

  - Wind-generated electricity increased by almost **21 percent** in 2007 over 2006, more than any other energy source. Solar power had the next greatest growth rate, growing by more than **19 percent** in 2007 over 2006.

  - **China** leads the world in the consumption of total renewable energy.

  - The **United States** is second, Canada is third, and Brazil is fourth in the consumption of total renewable energy.

# Giving Energy a Helping Hand

Many sources of energy are subsidized, or given money from the government to give them a leg up in the marketplace. Subsidies help an energy source get developed and compete with other sources, but also indicate a lack of stability.

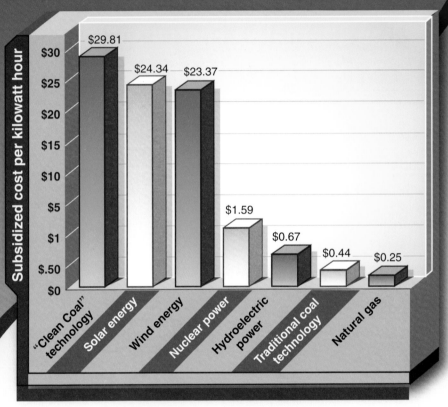

Source: Energy Information Administration, "Renewable Energy Consumption and Electricity Preliminary Statistics, 2007," 2008.

- According to the California Energy Commission and the Audubon Society:
  - Between **1,766 and 4,721 birds** are killed by wind turbines in California each year.
  - Between **456 and 1,129** of these are raptor species such as golden eagles, red-tailed hawks, American kestrels, and burrowing owls.

## Fuels That Power America

The United States relies heavily on fossil fuels, using them to satisfy more than 86 percent of its energy needs. In 2007 oil supplied more than 29 percent of the United States' total energy needs, while coal supplied 22 percent. Nuclear power supplied less than 9 percent and renewable sources supplied less than 7 percent of the nation's total energy.

| Energy Source | 2003 | 2004 | 2005 | 2006 | 2007 |
|---|---|---|---|---|---|
| **Fossil Fuels** | 84% | 85.8% | 85.8% | 84.6% | 86.2% |
| Coal | 22.3% | 22.4% | 22.7% | 22.4% | 22.7% |
| Coal Coke* Net Imports | 0.05% | 0.13% | 0.04% | 0.06% | 0.02% |
| Natural Gas | 22.8% | 22.9% | 22.5% | 22.1% | 23.6% |
| Petroleum | 38.8% | 40.2% | 40.3% | 39.9% | 39.8% |
| **Nuclear** | 7.9% | 8.2% | 8.1% | 8.2% | 8.4% |
| **Renewable** | 6.1% | 6.2% | 6.4% | 6.9% | 6.8% |
| Biomass | 2.8% | 3.0% | 3.1% | 3.3% | 3.6% |
| Biofuels | 0.4% | 0.5% | 0.5% | 0.7% | 1.0% |
| Waste | 0.4% | 0.3% | 0.4% | 0.4% | 0.4% |
| Wood-Derived Fuels | 2.0% | 2.1% | 2.1% | 2.1% | 2.1% |
| Geothermal | 0.331 | 0.3% | 0.3% | 0.3% | 0.3% |
| Hydroelectric | 2.825 | 2.6% | 2.7% | 2.8% | 2.4% |
| Solar/PV | 0.064 | 0.06% | 0.06% | 0.07% | 0.08% |
| Wind | 0.115 | 0.1% | 0.1% | 0.2% | 0.3% |
| **Total** | 98.2% | 100.3% | 100.5% | 99.8% | 101.6% |

Note: All numbers in percent; totals do not equal 100 percent due to rounding.
*a fuel derived from coal

Source: Energy Information Administration, "Renewable Energy Consumption and Electricity Preliminary Statistics 2007," 2008.

# Pushing Renewable Energy

Twenty-eight states have passed renewable energy porfolios (RPS), or laws that require a certain portion of the state's energy to come from renewable sources by a certain year. Five states have set a renewable energy goal.

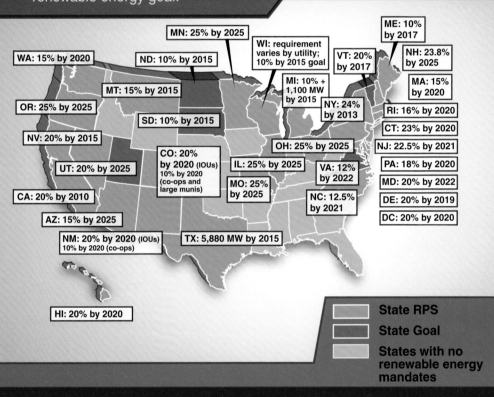

ME: 10% by 2017

MN: 25% by 2025

WI: requirement varies by utility; 10% by 2015 goal

VT: 20% by 2017

NH: 23.8% by 2025

WA: 15% by 2020

ND: 10% by 2015

MA: 15% by 2020

MT: 15% by 2015

MI: 10% + 1,100 MW by 2015

OR: 25% by 2025

NY: 24% by 2013

RI: 16% by 2020

SD: 10% by 2015

CT: 23% by 2020

NV: 20% by 2015

OH: 25% by 2025

NJ: 22.5% by 2021

CO: 20% by 2020 (IOUs) 10% by 2020 (co-ops and large munis)

IL: 25% by 2025

VA: 12% by 2022

PA: 18% by 2020

UT: 20% by 2025

MO: 25% by 2025

MD: 20% by 2022

CA: 20% by 2010

NC: 12.5% by 2021

DE: 20% by 2019

AZ: 15% by 2025

DC: 20% by 2020

NM: 20% by 2020 (IOUs) 10% by 2020 (co-ops)

TX: 5,880 MW by 2015

HI: 20% by 2020

State RPS

State Goal

States with no renewable energy mandates

Source: Interstate Renewable Energy Council, "Renewables Portfolio Standards," 2008.

- According to the Heritage Foundation, windmills have a life expectancy of about **20 years**, while nuclear power plants can produce power for up to **80 years**.

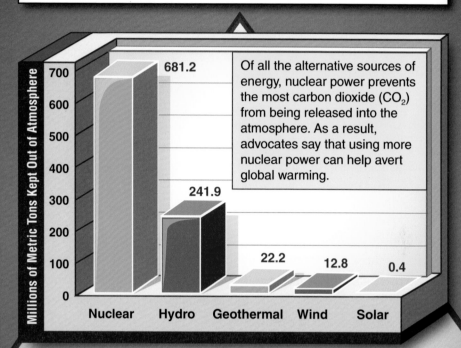

# Keeping CO$_2$ Out of the Atmosphere

Of all the alternative sources of energy, nuclear power prevents the most carbon dioxide (CO$_2$) from being released into the atmosphere. As a result, advocates say that using more nuclear power can help avert global warming.

**Millions of Metric Tons Kept Out of Atmosphere**

| |  |
|---|---|
| Nuclear | 681.2 |
| Hydro | 241.9 |
| Geothermal | 22.2 |
| Wind | 12.8 |
| Solar | 0.4 |

Source: Nuclear Energy Institute, "Nuclear Energy Plays Essential Role in Reducing Greenhouse Gas Emissions," July 2008. www.nei.org.

- There are five main forms of renewable energy: **solar**, **wind**, **water** (hydropower), **biofuels** (plant matter), and **geothermal** (heat from the earth).

- According to a March 2009 Gallup Poll:
  - **77 percent** of Americans think the government should offer more financial support and incentives for using renewable energy
  - **8 percent** of Americans think the government should offer less financial support and incentives for using renewable energy
  - **13 percent** of Americans think the government should not change the amount of financial support and incentives it offerse for using renewable energy
  - **3 percent** are unsure

# Key People and Advocacy Groups

**American Coalition for Clean Coal Electricity:** This group represents the coal industry's interest in promoting and pursuing clean coal technology and research.

**Julian Darley:** Darley is the founder of the Post Carbon Institute, a think tank that studies global reliance on cheap, carbon-based sources of energy. He is also the director of Global Public Media, which studies issues relating to peak oil production.

**Environmental Protection Agency:** The federal agency in charge of protecting the environment and controlling pollution. The agency works toward these goals by enacting and enforcing regulations, identifying and fining polluters, assisting businesses and local environmental agencies, and cleaning up polluted sites.

**Al Gore:** Gore was the forty-fifth vice president of the United States. Gore's 2006 documentary, *An Inconvenient Truth*, catapulted the issue of fossil fuels and climate change onto the international agenda. For his work, Gore received the Nobel Peace Prize in 2007.

**Marion King Hubbert:** Hubbert is a geoscientist who in 1956 developed the theory of peak oil, which states there is a point at which oil production will peak and then enter a state of permanent decline.

**Bjørn Lomborg:** Lomborg is a Danish author and professor best known for his book *The Skeptical Environmentalist*, which casts doubt on climate change, rejects the Kyoto Protocol, and opposes environmental alarmism.

**James Lovelock:** Lovelock is a British scientist who developed the Gaia hypothesis, which states that the Earth is a living, breathing organism. In 2004 Lovelock broke with fellow environmentalists when he became a fervent supporter of nuclear energy, claiming it was the only energy source capable of saving humanity from a climate catastrophe. He is a member of the group Environmentalists for Nuclear Energy.

**Patrick Moore:** Moore is a founding member of Greenpeace International, a prominent environmental group. Moore shocked fellow environmentalists when he became an ardent supporter of nuclear energy, billing it as a "green" energy source that should be promoted by environmentalists.

**Nuclear Energy Institute:** This is the policy organization of the nuclear energy industry; it promotes nuclear energy as a safe, clean, and cost-effective alternative to fossil fuels.

**Organization of Petroleum Exporting Countries (OPEC):** OPEC comprises Algeria, Angola, Ecuador, Iran, Iraq, Kuwait, Libya, Nigeria, Qatar, Saudi Arabia, the United Arab Emirates, and Venezuela. OPEC represents the interests of these oil-exporting nations and holds significant influence over oil production and the global oil market.

**David Pimental:** Pimental is a professor of agriculture and life sciences at Cornell University. He has been an outspoken voice against biofuels and believes they are unlikely to replace fossil fuels as an energy source.

# Chronology

**1956**
Geoscientist Marion King Hubbert predicts that that American oil supplies will peak in 1970 and the global oil supply will peak in 1999 or 2000.

**1815**
The first U.S. natural gas well is discovered.

**1951**
Saudi Arabia begins extracting oil from the Ghawar oil field, the largest oil field ever discovered.

**1908**
The first major oil strike in the Middle East takes place in Masjid-i-Suleiman, Iran.

**1800**     **1850**     **1900**     **1950**

**1917**
The United States is producing two-thirds of the world's oil supply.

**1927**
Oil is discovered near Kirkuk, Iraq, the first commercial find in any Arab country.

**1859**
The U.S. oil business is born in Titusville, Pennsylvania, when Edwin L. Drake strikes oil at 70 feet (21m).

**1960**
Iraq, Iran, Kuwait, Saudi Arabia, and Venezuela form the Organization of Petroleum Exporting Countries (OPEC).

Chronology

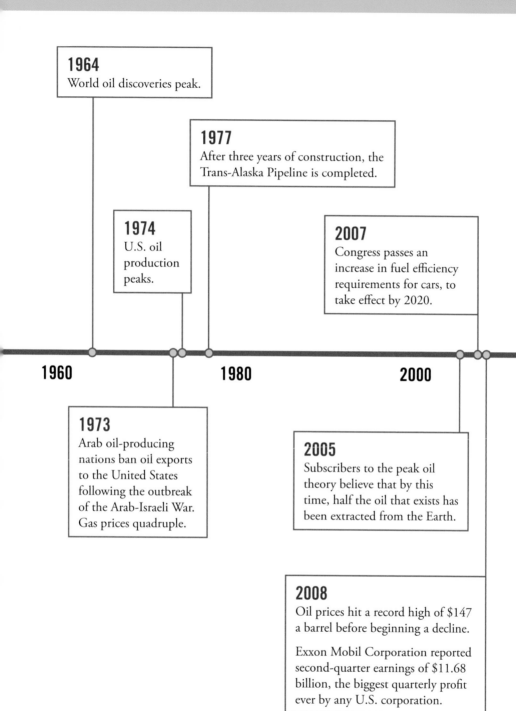

**1964**
World oil discoveries peak.

**1977**
After three years of construction, the Trans-Alaska Pipeline is completed.

**1974**
U.S. oil production peaks.

**2007**
Congress passes an increase in fuel efficiency requirements for cars, to take effect by 2020.

1960

1980

2000

**1973**
Arab oil-producing nations ban oil exports to the United States following the outbreak of the Arab-Israeli War. Gas prices quadruple.

**2005**
Subscribers to the peak oil theory believe that by this time, half the oil that exists has been extracted from the Earth.

**2008**
Oil prices hit a record high of $147 a barrel before beginning a decline.

Exxon Mobil Corporation reported second-quarter earnings of $11.68 billion, the biggest quarterly profit ever by any U.S. corporation.

# Related Organizations

### American Petroleum Institute (API)

1220 L St. NW

Washington, DC 20005

phone: (202) 682-8000

Web site: www.api.org

The API represents America's petroleum industry. Its activities include lobbying, conducting research, and setting technical standards for the petroleum industry. To this end, it publishes numerous position papers, reports, and information sheets.

### American Solar Energy Society (ASES)

2400 Central Ave., Suite G-1

Boulder, CO 80301

phone: (303) 443-3130 • fax (303) 443-3212

e-mail: ases@ases.org • Web site: www.ases.org

ASES promotes the use of solar energy. It disseminates information on solar energy to schools, universities, and communities.

### American Wind Energy Association (AWEA)

122 C. St. NW, Suite 380

Washington, DC 20001

phone: (202) 383-2500 • fax: (202) 383-2505

e-mail: windmail@awea.org • Web site: www.awea.org

The AWEA represents wind power plant developers, wind turbine manufacturers, utilities, consultants, insurers, financiers, researchers, and others involved in the wind industry. The association promotes the use of wind energy as a clean source of electricity for consumers around the world.

## Council on Alternative Fuels (CAF)

1225 Eye St. NW, Suite 320

Washington, DC 20005

phone: (202) 898-0711

CAF is a collection of companies interested in the production of synthetic fuels and the research and development of synthetic fuel technologies. It publishes information on new alternative fuels in the monthly publication *Alternate Fuel News*.

## Energy Conservation Coalition (ECC)

1525 New Hampshire Ave. NW

Washington, DC 20036

phone: (202) 745-4874

This group of public interest organizations promotes energy conservation. The ECC publishes *Powerline*, a bimonthly periodical covering consumer issues on energy and utilities.

## Environmental Protection Agency (EPA)

Ariel Rios Bldg.

1200 Pennsylvania Ave. NW

Washington, DC 20460

phone: (202) 272-0167

Web site: www.epa.gov

The EPA is the federal agency in charge of protecting the environment and controlling pollution. The agency works toward these goals by enacting and enforcing regulations, identifying and fining polluters, assisting businesses and local environmental agencies, and cleaning up polluted sites.

## Foundation for Clean Air Progress (FCAP)

1801 K St. NW, Suite 1000L

Washington, DC 20036

phone: (800) 272-1604

e-mail: info@cleanairprogress.org • Web site: www.cleanairprogress.org

This nonprofit organization promotes the progress that has been made in reducing air pollution. The foundation represents various sectors of business and industry in providing information to the public about improving air quality trends.

## Friends of the Earth

1025 Vermont Ave. NW, Suite 300

Washington, DC 20005

phone: (202) 783-7400

This group is dedicated to protecting the planet from environmental disaster and preserving biological diversity. As such, it supports energy policies that it believes are environmentally and socially responsible.

## The Intergovernmental Panel on Climate Change (IPCC)

c/o World Meteorological Organization, 7bis Ave. de la Paix

C.P. 2300, Geneva 2, Switzerland CH-1211

phone: + 41-22-730-8208

email: ipcc-sec@wmo.int • Web site: www.ipcc.ch

The IPCC was established by the United Nations in 1988 to assess the scientific, social, and economic information relevant to the understanding of the risk of human-induced climate change.

## International Association for Hydrogen Energy (IAHE)

PO Box 248266

Coral Gables, FL 3124

phone: (305) 284-4666

Web site: www.iahe.org

The IAHE is a group of scientists and engineers professionally involved with the production and use of hydrogen for fuel. It sponsors international forums to further its goal of creating an energy system based on hydrogen.

## National Biodiesel Board (NBB)

3337A Emerald Ln.

PO Box 104898

Jefferson City, MO 65110

phone: (573) 635-3893 • fax: (573) 635-7913

e-mail: info@biodiesel.org • Web site: www.biodiesel.org

The NBB represents the biodiesel industry and acts as the coordinating body for biodiesel research and development in the United States. It was founded in 1992 by state soybean commodity groups, who were funding biodiesel research and development programs.

## The National Renewable Energy Laboratory (NREL)

1617 Cole Blvd.

Golden, CO 80401-3393

phone: (303) 275-3000

Web site: www.nrel.gov

The NREL is the U.S. Department of Energy's laboratory for renewable energy research, development, and deployment, and a leading laboratory for energy efficiency. The laboratory's mission is to develop renewable energy and energy efficiency technologies and practices, to advance related science and engineering, and to transfer knowledge and innovations to address the nation's energy and environmental goals.

## Nuclear Energy Institute (NEI)

1776 Eye St. NW, Suite 400

Washington, DC 20006-3708

phone: (202) 739-8000 • fax: (202) 785-4019

e-mail: webmasterp@nei.org • Web site: www.nei.org

The NEI is the policy organization of the nuclear energy industry, whose objective is to promote policies that benefit the nuclear energy business.

### Renewable Energy Policy Project (REPP)

1612 K St. NW, Suite 202

Washington, DC 20006

phone: (202) 293-2898 • fax: (202) 298-5857

e-mail: info2@repp.org • Web site: www.repp.org

The REPP provides information about solar, hydrogen, biomass, wind, hydrogen, and other forms of renewable energy.

### Renewable Fuels Association (RFA)

1 Massachusetts Ave. NW, Suite 820

Washington, DC 20001

phone: (202) 289-3935 • fax: (202) 289-7519

e-mail: info@ethanolrfa.org • Web site: www.ethanolrfa.org

The RFA is made up of professionals who research, produce, and market renewable fuels, especially alcohol-based fuels such as ethanol.

### United Nations Environment Programme (UNEP)

United Nations Avenue, Gigiri

PO Box 30552, 00100

Nairobi, Kenya

phone: 254-2-7621234

e-mail: unepinfo@unep.org • Web site: www.unep.org

The mission of the UNEP is to provide leadership and encourage partnership in caring for the environment by inspiring, informing, and enabling nations and peoples to improve their quality of life without compromising that of future generations.

# For Further Research

## Books

David Craddock, *Renewable Energy Made Easy: Free Energy from Solar, Wind, Hydropower, and Other Alternative Energy Sources*. Ocala, FL: Atlantic, 2008.

Stan Gibilisco, *Alternative Energy Demystified*. New York: McGraw-Hill, 2006.

Jeff Goodell, *Big Coal: The Dirty Secret Behind America's Energy Future*. New York: Mariner, 2007.

Mark Jaccard, *Sustainable Fossil Fuels: The Unusual Suspect in the Quest for Clean and Enduring Energy*. New York: Cambridge University Press, 2006.

James R. Norman, *The Oil Card: Global Economic Warfare in the 21st Century*. Waterville, OR: TrineDay, 2008.

Dale Allen Pfeiffer, *Eating Fossil Fuels: Oil, Food and the Coming Crisis in Agriculture*. Gabriola Island, BC: New Society, 2006.

Elizabeth Raum, *Fossil Fuels and Biofuels*. Chicago: Heinemann, 2008.

Joe Shuster, *Beyond Fossil Fools: The Roadmap to Energy Independence by 2040*. Edina, MN: Beaver's Pond, 2008.

Robert Zubrin, *Energy Victory: Winning the War on Terror by Breaking Free of Oil*. Amherst, NY: Prometheus, 2007.

## Periodicals

Dennis T. Avery, "Saving Arctic Plant Species from Climate Change," *Hawaii Reporter*, May 21, 2008.

Jeff Biggers, "'Clean' Coal? Don't Try to Shovel That," *Washington Post*, March 2, 2008.

Paul Driessen, "Saving Lives with Coal," *Townhall*, January 3, 2008.

Ben Elgin, "The Dirty Truth About Clean Coal," *BusinessWeek*, June 19, 2008.

*Independent* (London), "World Oil Supplies Are Set to Run Out Faster than Expected, Warn Scientists," June 14, 2007.

Vasko Kohlmayer, "The Truth About Oil," *Front Page*, May 8, 2008.

Mark Lambrides and Juan Cruz Monticelli, "Illuminating the Power of Renewable Energy," *Americas*, May/June 2007.

Amy Leinbach Marquis, "Solar Rush," *National Parks Conservation Association Magazine*, Winter 2009.

Jim Lydecker, "Overpopulation and Peak Oil: The Perfect Storm," *Napa Valley Register*, January 18, 2008.

Janice Mason, "Arctic National Wildlife Refuge (ANWR): Why Not Drill in ANWR for Oil? Creating a Renewable Future," *Estes Park (CO) Trail-Gazette*, July 25, 2008.

Patrick Moore, "Nuclear & Green," *New York Post*, February 23, 2007.

Deroy Murdock, "Chill Out on Climate Hysteria: The Earth Is Currently Cooling," *National Review*, May 2, 2008.

Sherwood Ross, "Nuclear Power Not Clean, Green or Safe," *Political Affairs*, January 8, 2007.

John Scire, "Oil Dependency, National Security," *Nevada Appeal*, February 10, 2008.

## Internet Sources

Regina S. Axelrod, "Why Nuclear Energy May Not Be the Answer," International Relations and Security Network, April 26, 2007. www.isn.ethz.ch/isn/Digital-Library/Publications/Detail/?id=30596&lng=en.

Daniel Fine, "Oil Shale: Toward a Strategic Unconventional Fuels Supply Policy," Heritage Foundation, Lecture No. 1015, April 26, 2007. www.heritage.org/Research/EnergyandEnvironment/hl1015.cfm.

Jacob Leibenluft, "What the Heck Is 'Clean Coal?'" *Slate*, October 7, 2008. www.slate.com/id/2201661.

Joseph Romm, "Nuclear Bomb," *Salon*, June 2, 2008. http://www.salon.com/news/feature/2008/06/02/nuclear_power_price/index.html.

David B. Sandalow, "Ending Oil Dependence: Protecting National Security, the Environment, and the Economy," Brookings Institution, 2008. www.brookings.edu/~/media/Files/Projects/Opportunity08/PB_Energy_Sandalow.pdf.

Jack Spencer and Nicolas Loris, "Dispelling Myths About Nuclear Energy," *Backgrounder*, Heritage Foundation, December 3, 2007. www.heritage.org/Research/EnergyandEnvironment/upload/bg_2087.pdf.

## Web Sites

**Alliance to Save Energy** (www.ase.org)

**Office of Fossil Energy Homepage** (www.fossil.energy.gov)

**Organization of Petroleum Exporting Countries** (www.opec.org)

**Terror-Free Oil Initiative** (www.terrorfreeoil.org)

**The Coming Global Oil Crisis** (www.oilcrisis.com)

**World Without Oil** (http://worldwithoutoil.org)

# Source Notes

## Overview

1. Jim Lydecker, "Overpopulation and Peak Oil: The Perfect Storm," *Napa Valley Register*, January 18, 2008. www.napavalleyregister.com.
2. Peyton Knight, "ANWR: To Drill or Not to Drill? There Is No Question," National Policy Analysis No. 535, National Center for Public Policy Research, December 2005. www.nationalcenter.org.
3. Ariel Cohen, "The National Security Consequences of Oil Dependency," Heritage Foundation, Lecture No. 1021, May 14, 2007. www.heritage.org.
4. David B. Sandalow, "Rising Oil Prices, Declining National Security," Brookings Institution, May 22, 2008. www.brookings.edu.
5. Michael Pollen, *The Omnivore's Dilemma*. New York: Penguin, 2006, p. 182.
6. Pollen, *The Omnivore's Dilemma*, pp. 182–83.
7. Dale Allen Pfeiffer, "Eating Fossil Fuels," From the Wilderness, 2004. www.fromthewilderness.com.
8. Simon Usborne, "Plastic: Past, Present and Endangered Future," *Independent* (UK), May 16, 2007. www.independent.co.uk.
9. Richard Girard, "Why the Oil Industry Benefits from Bottled Water Sales," Global Policy Forum, June 26, 2008. www.globalpolicy.org.
10. Lydecker, "Overpopulation and Peak Oil."

## Is the World Running Out of Fossil Fuels?

11. Quoted in "World Oil Supplies Are Set to Run Out Faster than Expected, Warn Scientists," *Independent* (London), June 14, 2007. www.independent.co.uk.
12. Joseph Romm, "Peak Oil? Consider It Solved," *Salon*, March 28, 2008. www.salon.com.
13. Lydecker, "Overpopulation and Peak Oil."
14. Donald L. Gautier and Brenda S. Pierce, "Circum-Arctic Resource Appraisal: Estimates of Undiscovered Oil and Gas North of the Arctic Circle," U.S. Department of the Interior, July 23, 2008. http://energy.usgs.gov.
15. Vasko Kohlmayer, "The Truth About Oil," *Front Page*, May 8, 2008. www.frontpagemag.com.
16. Kohlmayer, "The Truth About Oil."
17. Kohlmayer, "The Truth About Oil."
18. U.S. Geological Survey, "Circum-Arctic Resource Appraisal: Estimates of Undiscovered Oil and Gas North of the Arctic Circle," USGS Fact Sheet 2008–3049, July 23, 2008, p. 1. http://pubs.usgs.gov.
19. Daniel Fine, "Oil Shale: Toward a Strategic Unconventional Fuels Supply Policy," Heritage Foundation, Lecture #1015, April 26, 2007. www.heritage.org.
20. Friends Committee on National Legislation, "Oppose Environmentally Harmful Alternative Fuels Amendments to DOD Authorization Bill (Senate)," May 7, 2008. www.fcnl.org.
21. Romm, "Peak Oil? Consider It Solved."

## Does Fossil Fuel Use Threaten the Environment?

22. Intergovernmental Panel on Climate Change, "Climate Change 2007: Sum-

mary for Policymakers," 2007, p. 6. www.ipcc.ch.

23. Quoted in John M. Broder, "Obama Affirms Climate Change Goals," *New York Times*, November 18, 2008. www.nytimes.com.

24. Dennis T. Avery, "Saving Arctic Plant Species from Climate Change," *Hawaii Reporter*, May 21, 2008. www.hudson.org.

25. "Open Letter to the Secretary-General of the United Nations," December 13, 2007. www.heartland.org.

26. Paul Driessen, "Saving Lives with Coal," *Townhall*, January 3, 2008. http://townhall.com.

27. Jacob Leibenluft, "What the Heck Is 'Clean Coal?'" *Slate*, October 7, 2008. www.slate.com.

28. Quoted in Diane Silver, "Celebrate Clean Coal, Come On!" *Salon*, May 15, 2008. www.salon.com.

29. Quoted in "McCain Delivers Remarks on Energy and Economic Policy," *Washington Post*, June 18, 2008. www.washingtonpost.com.

30. Ben Elgin, "The Dirty Truth About Clean Coal," *BusinessWeek*, June 19, 2008. www.businessweek.com.

31. Quoted in Elgin, "The Dirty Truth About Clean Coal."

32. Elgin, "The Dirty Truth About Clean Coal."

33. Jeff Biggers, "'Clean' Coal? Don't Try to Shovel That," *Washington Post*, March 2, 2008, p. B02. www.washingtonpost.com.

## How Does Fossil Fuel Use Affect National Security?

34. John Scire, "Oil Dependency, National Security," *Nevada Appeal*, February 10, 2008. www.nevadaappeal.com.

35. Quoted in APS Diplomat News Service, "Zawahiri Urges Attacks on Gulf Oil Sites; Sees in Iraq 'Catastrophe'

for USA," December 12, 2005.

36. Michael T. Klare, "Oil: The Real Threat to National Security," *Salon*, October 4, 2004. www.salon.com.

37. David B. Sandalow, "Ending Oil Dependence: Protecting National Security, the Environment, and the Economy," Brookings Institution, 2008. www.brookings.edu.

38. Scire, "Oil Dependency, National Security."

39. Klare, "Oil."

40. Joe Bell, "Follow the Facts and Drill in ANWR," Opinioneditorials.com, November 10, 2005. www.opinioneditorials.com.

41. Jerry Taylor and Peter Van Doren, "Driving Bin Laden? Oil Consumption Has Little to Do with Terrorism," *National Review*, March 8, 2006. www.nationalreview.com.

42. Taylor and Van Doren, "Driving Bin Laden? Oil Consumption Has Little to Do with Terrorism."

## Can Alternative Energy Sources Replace Fossil Fuels?

43. Peter W. Huber and Mark P. Mills, "Why the U.S. Needs More Nuclear Power," *City Journal*, Winter 2005. www.city-journal.org.

44. Jack Spencer and Nicolas Loris, "Dispelling Myths About Nuclear Energy," *Backgrounder*, Heritage Foundation, December 3, 2007. www.heritage.org.

45. Patrick Moore, "Nuclear & Green," *New York Post*, February 23, 2007. www.nypost.com.

46. Quoted in Elsa Wenzel, "Nuke Power Not So Green or Clean," CNET News, June 11, 2007. http://news.cnet.com.

47. Sherwood Ross, "Nuclear Power Not Clean, Green or Safe," *Political Affairs*, January 8, 2007. www.politicalaffairs.net.

48. Regina S. Axelrod, "Why Nuclear Energy May Not Be the Answer," International Relations and Security Network, April 26, 2007. www.isn.ethz.ch.

49. Spencer and Loris, "Dispelling Myths About Nuclear Energy."

50. Joseph Romm, "Nuclear Bomb," *Salon*, June 2, 2008. www.salon.com.

51. Amy Leinbach Marquis, "Solar Rush," *National Parks*, Winter 2009. www.npca.org.

# List of Illustrations

# Index

# About the Author

Lauri S. Friedman earned her bachelor's degree in religion and political science from Vassar College in 1999. She is the founder of LSF Editorial, a writing and editing shop in San Diego. Her clients include Reference-Point Press, for whom she has written *The Death Penalty, Nuclear Weapons and Security, Terrorist Attacks, Abortion, Islam,* and *Assisted Suicide,* all in the Compact Research series. Friedman lives in Ocean Beach, San Diego, with her husband, Randy, and their yellow lab, Trucker.